Gloria Klein

A Metaphysical and Anecdotal Consideration of the Fart

Gloria Klein

Gloria Klein

Gloria Klein

© 2014

Alphabeta Press
DES PLAINES, Illinois

e: RKleinEngler@aol.com

Special thanks to Micheal Cromley
of Afton, Michigan

and Robert Klein Engler
of Chicago, Illinois

9th Inflated Edition

Gloria Klein

Gloria Klein

.CONTENTS.

Gloria Klein

Gloria Klein

A Metaphysical and Anecdotal
Consideration of the Fart

Gloria Klein

Gloria Klein

A Metaphysical and Anecdotal Consideration of the Fart

sed quamuis sibi caverit crepando,
compressis natibus Iouem salutat.

--Martial, LXXVII

What seems at first to be an innocent or inconspicuous remark, upon reflection, often lays bare the fabric of reality. Such is the case as I settle down to a lunch of cabbage and beans. I notice the wind is picking up. Outside, the hot hours of an August afternoon in Chicago give way to gusty thunderstorms. The stereo is playing the last few bars of Otmar Nussio's "Divertimento for Contrabassoon." I can't help think, as a car backfires in the street below, of what I had just read in an advice column of the local newspaper. It was an article about farting and politeness. The more I think about that article, the more I believe the advice columnist had one of her rare lapses of judgment. She advised that it is not polite to fart in public.

Anyone who gives this advice a moment's thought realizes the obvious--most people fart nowhere else but in public. Because we fart in public, we ought to accept the public fart, yet as far back as the fourteenth century we read such warnings as "Beware of thy hinder parts from gunblasting." A more civilized approach to farting is certainly to be found in ancient Rome. Need we be reminded that the Roman emperor Claudius, being so alarmed at the prospect of someone dying while attempting to stifle a fart, he considered issuing an imperial decree making it permissible to fart at the dinner table?

It's a sad commentary on our times, that modern man has not learned from the ancient Romans. We are still trying to stifle the fart. Chuck Shepherd reports in his column, "News of the Weird," printed in the Chicago Reader for April, 1994, about efforts to prevent farting in professional sports. Professional soccer team manager Dan O'Riordan, defending his decision to levy fines against players for flatulence in the locker room, reportedly said, "It can get fairly oppressive when you've got 20 players in a tiny dressing room all suffering the effects of a Sunday night curry." Then there is the statement from the Swedish hockey team's coach Curt Lundmark. The coach was discussing why he didn't protest more vigorously a disallowed goal in a game between his team and Canada's in February at the 1994 Olympics. "Sweden's influence in international hockey is like a duck fart in Africa," he said matter of factly.

If we can't stifle the fart, then we attempt to "cure" it by various remedies. How many of these remedies have come and gone, been forgotten in time the way we have forgotten that bottle of Angostura Bitters many of us keep in our refrigerator for years? If one is troubled by too many farts, just read the recommendation in fine print found on the label: "For flatulence, one to four teaspoonfuls after meals."

The simple remedy of bitters may have been overlooked by Benjamin Franklin. In his Letter to the Royal Academy of Brussels, Franklin writes, "He that dines on stale Flesh, especially with much addition of Onions shall be able to afford a stink that no company can tolerate." It may be because of too much flesh and onions that Franklin proposed, "My prize question therefore should be: To discover some Drug, wholesome and not disagreeable, to be mixed with our common food, or sauce, that shall render the natural discharge of Wind from our bodies not only inoffensive, but agreeable as Perfumes." If we had such a drug, no one would be bothered by holding a fart to let it go in private. Just the opposite, we would look forward to them as lovers look for roses.

And who is to say there is not already a remedy for farting? The other day a colleague of mine, well aware of the direction my research was taking, passed on to me a roll of Dr. Fozwanger's Anti-Fart Tablets. This product, manufactured by The Comic Relief Company of St. Louis, claims to "snuff out the stinkiest of those stinkers!" It is produced for chronic farters who, according to the label, find themselves trying to "squeeze one out quietly." Could this be what Mr. Franklin was looking for so many years ago in colonial America? Or would he say it was not worth a "FARThing."

Of more value is a product sold now at many drugstores. Beano could be a more reliable alternative to Franklin's drug. The ingredient in this little plastic squeeze bottle is supposed to solve the problem of farting. Just a few drops of this natural liquid on food such as beans or cabbage, and embarrassed and suffering farters can eat to their hearts content. The manufacturer claims Beano helps dissolve the complex sugars that ferment into gas in the intestine. They describe it as a scientific and social breakthrough. Beano relieves the eater of the social and personal discomfort of too much intestinal gas. The only caution is that the product should not be used on food that is too warm. Let your plate of beans cool a little before baptizing it, but don't expect the smell of roses later.

An informant tells me the company making Beano is also going to market a product for preventing dog farts. It will be called Curtail and can be placed in the dog's food. By using Curtail, your dog can eat as many beans as it likes. You won't have to worry about it embarrassing you in front of the neighbors.

Certainly, a product like Beano would be welcome "down under" in Sydney, Australia. There, they like to eat pea pies made with a locally grown pea that is fondly referred to as a "blue blaster." Incidentally, the Australian government has also set aside money to study the effect of farting on the hole in the ozone layer.

Other products besides Beano have come to the aid of flatulent suffers. INNERMINT is an internal deodorant caplet with 100 mg of concentrated Chlorophyl. The ad copy for the product claims, "It works to deodorize the body from the inside! It's safe, natural, simple to swallow, and if used as part of a regular personal hygiene routine, will restore your confidence as it eliminates foul odors." If all this is believed, "the consumer may save over 25% off the already reduced 2 bottle price if you arrange for automatic shipments of INNERMINT every 60 days for an amazingly low price of $10.95 per bottle. No minimum obligation, shipping is free after initial order and you may cancel at anytime by calling 1-866-MINTPILL."

Modern Americans have not given up their questions about farts and a cure just because there are products on the market that claim to deal with too much gas in the digestive track. Recently, a new 900 telephone number became available to offer medical advice. According to an article in the July 22, 1991, issue of Time magazine, one of the four most common questions asked by callers was, "Why do I always have gas?" For the answer, call 1-900-7DOCTOR.

Perhaps the help of medical science is too drastic a step. Maybe you prefer a more natural solution to the problem of flatulence. The other day a "Gas Pass" came into my hands that permits you to have your wish. This red, white and blue card is the size of a credit card and is a farting permit officially signed by president G. U. Stink. The back of the card encourages the holder to "Keep this card handy and feel free to make use of the following types of excuses: Blame-It-On-The-Doggie-Fart, Lingering Limburger, Vapor Choke, or All of the Above." These excuses are not valid, however, until the card bearer signs with an authorized signature.

And if this is not enough, there is also a product called "Fart Powder," made in England by Bristol Novelty, Ltd., that does what its name implies. The directions read: "Put the powder into a hot drink and retreat to a safe distance. Not recommended for children under eight years." No telephone number is listed.

What if you or someone you loved were a victim to such an unfortunate prank and actually consumed some "Fart

Powder." Would they be encouraged to hold out as long as they could? I don't know many people who can hold a fart until they are in a private location. The amount of vapor along with the force of gas pressure in the bowels often renders the task impossible. Besides, at least one researcher, G. Waynne-Jones, writing in the medical journal Lancet (1975), has suggested that "Flatus Retention is the Major Factor in Diverticular Disease." This agrees with advice from the medical school at Salerno in the eleventh century. The doctors there wrote, "Those who suppress farts risk dropsy, convulsions, vertigo, and frightful colics."

Such advice was echoed in the eighteen century as well. Writing in 1712, in his book A Cruising Voyage Round the World, Woodes Rogers tells us about the adventures of Alexander Selkirk. Selkirk was cast away on the isolated island of Juan Fernandez. "He found there also a black pepper called Malagita, which was very good to expel wind and against griping of the guts." Perhaps it was knowledge of this plant that got Charles Darwin in trouble. We learn from Janet Browne's Charles Darwin, A Biography, Volume One: Voyaging, that besides being a bad speller (writing Barrow

Cooter - for barracuda) it was a problem with farting that led Darwin to leave social meals early.

Were these men granted insight into what research shows has been known for centuries? Holding your wind just isn't healthy. Why was a man like Darwin so squeamish, leaving meals early just because of a fart? Perhaps those farts were rock-shivering blasts instead of little putters, and the embarrassment was as great as the announcement. Nowadays the syndicated columnist Cecil Adams opines sane advice when he ignores old conventions and writes, "When in doubt, let it out." Furthermore, there just isn't enough time in our busy lives to wait to fart in private. Your average fart is the public fart. A moment's reflection on farting is enough to persuade anyone that the commandment not to fart in public is too difficult to follow.

Perhaps one of the best courses of action to take when faced with an immanent fart, is to slide politely away from the truth, and dismiss yourself. Southern women used to speak of "having the vapors." When the vapors came upon them, they requested permission to retire to another room. In the humid south, with the odors of the swamp wafting through the doors of the big house, who would not grant them such?

"But wait," some resident liberal might interrupt, "this concern about how and where to fart is not a universal one." The problem of holding a fart is not one of the worries several million people with ileostomies wring their hands over. They don't have to worry about farts, because their gas goes silently into a bag and is released in private. Before we dwell on those who worry about farting, let's take note of those who don't.

I have a friend with such an ileostomy. When she smells a fart she thinks that her bag is leaking. In reality, it is someone else who let a fart nearby, her bag being secure. Since she stopped farting, she can no longer tolerate the aromas of someone else's nature. Thus she warns her boyfriends not to drink beer when they come over. How much this lack of tolerance is related to the fact that her father used to torture her mother in bed by farting and holding the blankets over her head is difficult to determine.

Astronauts also do not fart in public--when they are sealed in their space suits, that is. It may come as a surprise to some, but NASA spent quite a lot of money trying to solve the problem of farts in space. A special diet was developed and a special design incorporated into the survival suits of astronauts because we humans do fart a lot. In outer space this must be kept to a minimum. Besides the odor, in zero gravity, a good fart is also a source of propulsion. Too many beans, and astronauts can send themselves into orbit.

Nevertheless, with the exception of those with illeostomies and those who fart in space suits, most of us fart in public all the time. This fact leads to the conclusion that the real etiquette of farting is that you must not fart loudly in public. That man on the elevated train who bends down to pick up the umbrella he dropped and unintentionally emits a roll of thunder, as if Zeus had spoken, along with as noxious an odor as we would get at the rim of a sulfur pit, that man is rude and an embarrassment. If he could just let his fart slide out, all would be well.

We would still have to suffer the aroma, but we do that in silence all the time anyway. It is not the smell but the noise we must consider when we discuss the manners of farting. The polite fart is the quiet fart. Except, of course, in a public toilet, where often, in the stall next to you, you hear the rumble and splatter of the remains of some god-awful meal tumbling down to the watery depths, followed by a groan of satisfaction that makes you hurry up your own business and get out of there before the stink hits.

Farting loudly in public cannot only ruin one's social life, it can also ruin one's career. Take the case of the Argentinean ambassador to Great Britain, Juan Berger. In 1895 he was acquitted of murdering his doctor, Carlos Aguilar, by a jury that understood all too well the problems of loud farts in public. Though found innocent, he nevertheless had to give up his ambassadorship and his life in public. It seems that the ambassador went under the knife of the good doctor to have some hemorrhoids corrected. The knife slipped and the ambassador's rectum was injured. He recovered, but it was soon discovered that his sphincter muscle was damaged, and he no longer had control over it. Farts would escape him at any time, often when the ambassador was in the most delicate and diplomatic situations. As he bowed before the queen, rose to toast the President of Argentina, bent over to pick up the dropped glove of a debutante, all of a sudden, a long drawn out announcement from the nether regions rolled forth. This being too much to take, he got a pistol and shot the doctor whose hand was the cause of his embarrassment and loss of station. After a long trial, which took its toll, he appeared in the courtroom flaco como pedito de víbora, "thin as a snake's fart," as they say in Argentina, to await the verdict. The jury agreed with his motives and freed him. I understand he was heard sputtering as he left the courthouse.

More recently, a loud fart actually contributed to another man's death. In this incident it was the farter and not the fartee, however. The police in Pueblo, Colorado, charged Daniel Serna, nineteen, with murdering Robert Vinci in June of 1990. Mr. Serna and a friend were standing in front of a 7-Eleven minimart when Vinci rode up on his bike and farted in front of the two. Vinci smiled and said, "I've been ripping them all day." Serna replied with, "Well, don't be ripping them in front of me." A fight ensued, and Serna allegedly pulled a gun and shot Vinci.

Perhaps this tragic incident might not have happened if the police had gotten to Vinci earlier. A few weeks later, the same newspaper column reported that a Baylor University freshman, Kyle Krebs, was ticketed by campus police in April of 1991 for breaking wind in violation of a campus ordinance prohibiting obnoxious odors. Krebs argued he was not directing his farts at the police, "They were so far away, and cars were driving by. I never thought the decibel level would be so high he would hear it." Thank God the officer did. If that behavior were permitted to continue, Kyle might have joined Vinci in the hereafter.

It seems the fart has been used as an insult throughout history. Josephus, in his *Bellum Judaicum* relates an incident from the first century of such a fart. It occurred at the time when the Romans were occupying Jerusalem, just before the outbreak of the Jewish war. "The people had assembled in Jerusalem for the Feast of Unleavened Bread, and the Roman cohort stood on guard over the Temple colonnade, armed men always being on duty at the feasts to forestall any rioting by the vast crowds. One of the soldiers pulled up his garment and bent over indecently, turning his backside towards the Jews and making a noise as indecent as his attitude. This infuriated the whole crowd, who noisily appealed to Cumanus to punish the soldier, while the less restrained of the young men and the naturally tumultuous section of the people rushed into battle, and snatching up stones, hurled them at the soldiers.... So violently did the dense mass struggle to escape that they trod on each other, and more than 30,000 were crushed. Thus the feast ended in distress to the whole nation and bereavement to every household." All this, because of a fart, which, if we are to take Josephus at face value, must have been quite a loud and rumbling one.

Then there is the case of the tell tale fart. This fart was not so loud as that of a Roman soldier nor as destructive to human life, but it did tell more than it was supposed to. In October 1994, the New York Daily News reported on an incident where a man known as a "career criminal" was apprehended in the middle of a burglary at an upscale Fire Island home. The residents had been awakened by noises but found no one until they heard farts coming from behind a closet door. Hiding inside the closet was the burglar, who was detained by the residents until police arrived. We can only imagine the resident of this house as gay, but if they were gay, is this another good argument for not remaining in the closet?

Farts can disturb the equilibrium of the talented and educated as well. Garrison Keiler claims in his piece *A Young Lutheran Guide to the Orchestra* that, "A bad note on a French Horn is like passing wind at a funeral." Yet, there is more to the problem than just bad notes. The general manager of the Kansas City Symphony reportedly suspended an oboe player after he made a "facetious response" to a complaint about him. The general manager had told him that a horn player complained that, during a rehearsal for The Nutcracker, the oboe player had passed gas in a loud manner, "creating an overpowering smell." To prevent this, the oboe player was suspended. This, no doubt, gave him more time to enjoy his favorite lunch of chile and beans, and the orchestra an opportunity to consider the relative value of wood winds over brass.

The cases above, and especially the one of Kyle and Vinci, might cause someone to ask if a person has ever died of a fart attack? In a recent novel by Laura Esquirel, Like Water for Chocolate, we find an answer to our question. A Mexican writer, familiar with the effects of beans and chilies, Esquirel has one of her characters, Rosaura, suffer an untimely fate.

She first complains to her sister of bad breath and gas. "For some weeks now she was having serious digestive problems.... All these ills carried with them an infinity of problems, the worst being that every day Pedro (her husband) moved farther and farther away from her...even she couldn't stand the foul smell."

Eventually, the fateful day arrived. Pedro had gone upstairs to say good night to Rosaura before going to sleep (he now has his own room). "At first Pedro didn't find it odd that he could hear Rosaura breaking wind even with the door closed. He began to notice the unpleasant noise when one lasted so long it seemed it would never end. The floor was shaking, the light blinked off and on. Maybe it was the engine of one of the neighbor's motor cars. How strange that he could smell it even though he'd taken the precaution of walking all around the bedroom with a spoon containing a chunk of burning charcoal and a pinch of sugar." Worried, Pedro goes into Rosaura's bedroom and finds her dead. Included in Esquirel's book is a nice recipe for beans with chili, Tezcucana-style.

Farts heard in public seem to have a strange effect on some people. Consider a recent case in Chesterfield Township, Michigan. There a thirty-six year old man was charged with assault and battery after brandishing a rifle and barricading himself in his home with his wife and son and a family friend. What could be the cause of such extreme action? Police said the affair started when the ten year old son became flatulent while watching TV. The boy's father got angry, first at the boy, then at the wife and friend when they defended the child.

Besides the social disruption of farts documented in the above cases, the very gas from fart emissions can be dangerous in some situations. An incident in Perth, Australia, confirms this. In July of 1991, a man picked up by an ambulance eventually caused the evacuation of both the ambulance and two hospital emergency rooms. He was uncontrollably emitting poisonous fumes from his anus and other body openings due to industrial-strength pesticides he had swallowed. Talk about problems down under!

Of course the above examples are extreme. Most people are not killed by farts, they are just embarrassed. The popular

TV sitcom Roseanne had an episode about the daughter of the family who found herself in an embarrassing situation brought on by a fart. She was humiliated at her high school when she farted in class while giving a speech. Her boyfriend, overcoming social pressures, nevertheless went to her house to keep the date he made with her, thus proving a fart would not keep them apart. The actual fart, however, which was the cause of much embarrassment, was not broadcast to a national TV audience. It was only related in dialogue with other members of the family. Too bad, for it would have been interesting to hear what kind of fart it was.

In the 1973 Mel Brooks film Blazing Saddles, there is also a humorous scene about cowboys sitting around a campfire eating beans and farting. These are not real farts we hear. They are Hollywood generated sound effects. It's like making the sound of a galloping horse by pounding on your chest. In the movie, Ski Patrol, we likewise hear some Hollywood generated farts from a dog who has a gas problem. His farts are heard and commented on by the characters in the film, but most of the jokes are cheap shots.

The farting dog also plays a role in the 1992 film *Kuffs*. In his review of the film titled, "When in doubt, have the dog break wind," Scott Collins remarks, "The makers of *Kuffs* are pleased to bring you another proud moment in American cinema: Trapped in a basement where a bomb is about to explode, our young hero turns to his dog for help, at which point the pooch loudly passes gas." It seems the dog had a bomb of its own.

It is by cheap shots like those above that Hollywood constantly deceives the public. They are almost as bad as the joke which asks what's the difference between a gay man and a refrigerator? The questionable answer is that the refrigerator doesn't fart when you take the meat out. With humor like this you can understand my disappointment when I heard about the film, Backdraft. Expecting an illustrated history of the fart in technicolor, the movie turned out to be just another story about firemen and fires.

It is not only Hollywood that uses farts as a cheap shot in movies. The Europeans are catching on to the symbolic and comic effects of farts in feature films. In the 1990 film, Evenings, by the Dutch director Rudolf Van den Berg, we come to hate the father of the hero because of his bad habits of farting and not using the sugar bowl properly. There is no way, however, to tell from the credits if the farts we hear on screen are real human farts imported from Europe or just ordinary sound effects.

AOL, the computer service accessible by modem and telephone line, offers its subscribers many files and programs that can be downloaded free of charge. Among them are a HyperCard cartoon of a farting man and various fart sounds that can be incorporated into the programing of the Macintosh computer. Such sounds as MegaFart, Relieved and Big Fart Noise are available. Each takes about a minute or two for downloading, depending on the speed of your modem, and is digitized for use at home. They can be incorporated into documents to give an editorial opinion, used as an alert when a program is running, or best of all, as a start up sound.

Just imagine, turning on your computer and hearing a fart. This might just be the safety device those with flatulence in a crowed office need to divert attention from their moment of crisis. Nevertheless, all we get from the computer is the noise; the smell must certainly wait for further advances in computer science. Furthermore, because these are computer generated sounds, we have to leave it up to the listener to decide if they carry all the tone, resonance and impact of an actual live fart.

The ever changing vocabulary of farts has also reached the computer age. There is now a new use for old terms. Consider the following definitions available through the Internet's online dictionary of computer terms.

memory farts: n. The flatulent sounds that some DOS box BIOSes (most notably AMIs) make when checking memory on bootup.

old fart: n. Tribal elder. A title self-assumed with remarkable frequency by (esp.) USENETters who have been programming for more than about 25 years; often appears in {sig block}s attached to Jargon File contributions of great archeological significance. This is a term of insult in the second or third person but one of pride in the first person.

The only media record of a real human fart I know about is one that occurs in the second of a series of male porno films produced under the "Old Reliable" label. In that video there is recorded an off-screen fart by one of the male models.

Outside of that, TV, film and radio producers are reluctant to incorporate the sound of real farts in broadcasts.

I suspect they subscribe to the general etiquette that the broadcast fart is a loud fart. They argue that a fart heard is a fart too loud. No TV producer wants to be the first to break with convention on this one. Maybe when they do get the courage, they can begin coverage of farting by what I consider to be one of the most notable exceptions to the rule prohibiting loud farting in public. As one would suspect, this exception takes place at the seat of learning, that is to say, on many American university campuses. There it is permissible to fart in public, if it is done as part of that primitive fraternity ritual called simply "lighting a fart."

I was present once at such a ritual and can describe it for you. The farter, usually a young man who has had too many beers, is first goaded by his brothers. They all then pass to a darkened room where he drops his pants and shorts and falls on his back with his legs spread and raised to a position with which many gay men are familiar. Either he or someone else holds a Bic lighter or a live match near his asshole and when he farts, methane, one of the chief components of a fart, ignites, creating a momentary blue flame to the joy and shouts of his comrades. Those who have seen this light in a darkened room say its color is a metaphor for love.

The lighting of farts does not often end with such insight. In Chuck Shepherd's column, "News of the Weird," published in the Chicago Reader for September 6th, 1991, we read of a case where fart lighting lead to death. Arlene Evans argued before the Kansas Court of Appeals that her husband did not commit suicide. Though he was found in his bathtub, clothed and charred, she said it was an accident that he died. Her husband was a heavy smoker and had often burned himself. Her strongest argument was that he often struck matches after farting, to burn off the smell. The fire that killed him in fact started around his crotch. The court believed her and ordered the insurance company to pay up.

Heavy drinking and farting rituals, like those described above, sooner or later lead to farting contests. In the early sixties, Laugh Records issued a recording of a humorous sketch depicting such a contest. They titled it, "The Crepitation Contest." Copies of those recordings are still circulated, but the artists and writer remain anonymous. It is worth the effort to track down a copy of this record to discover the awful fate of Lord Windermere. On records like that, one may also hear such jokes as, "What do you get from eating a dish of baked beans and onions?" Tear gas.

There is another record put out by Natural Gas, Ltd., Box 566, Massean, New York, which goes much farther in documenting the musical qualities of farts. Besides referring to farting contests that go back to the reign of King George I in 1732, they actually include songs that have long since become famous. "Down at the Old Bull and Bush" is a good example. The liner notes claim this is a state-of-the-art recording using microphones designed by one of Germany's leading microphone manufactures. To capture the transient impact and overtone structure of live farts, a stereo microphone was placed at floor level. The recording location was the famous Maple Leaf Garden at Toronto, Canada. The site was chosen not for acoustical reasons but rather for the excellent ventilation and air circulating system used in the Garden.

There is no way of knowing for sure if the farts recorded on both records are actually "real" farts and not just sound effects. We just have to take them at their word. I like to think we are in the presence of real talent here. Just the fact that Natural Gas, Ltd., documented the feat that General Cornwallis held the record for the greatest number of fudgie farts in succession for nearly 100 years is worth the price of purchase.

Concerns over farting in public are not limited to college students and the young people who buy fart records. The other side of academia, the faculty, also suffers from the effects of public farts. Recently, at the college where the author teaches, an incident over classroom farts was blown all out of proportion. To quote from a letter sent to the Dean of Students by the concerned faculty member: "On Friday, while having 'Fun' in the classroom, he (a student in the class) in a very loud manner passed gas thereby creating a great amount of commotion and disruption. Passing gas in that manner was obviously funny to him because he smiled after doing it. (Ah, relief?) There is absolutely no sane reason why I or other students in the classroom should have to inhale someone's foul and stinking odor while indulging in the educational process. I have had enough, please deal with this matter immediately."

A meeting of the college disciplinary board was convened. The student involved in the incident came with a letter from his doctor establishing an intestinal disorder. The faculty member did not show up to press his complaint. The board concluded that to bring this student in contact with that professor was an explosive combination. Eventually, the board realized something was in the air, and the winds of compromise prevailed. The matter was dismissed with a warning to the student to be polite. So far, good manners have prevailed.

According to my informant about most things academic, Micheal Cromley, this incident at the college represents just the tip of the iceberg. "There's more hot air where that came from," says Cromley. He has complied a unique collection of scatological documents over the years and will testify at length as to the peculiar interest academics have in the end products of students and other faculty members.

Thankfully, most of us never tell stories about farts or are called to testify before disciplinary committees about the farts we hear. Neither are we involved in farting rituals or contests, where we have to make sure our fart is seen and heard. After we fart quietly in public there is another rule of etiquette we try to follow, and that is: the quiet fart is also followed by the not-too-loud denial. After the fart, if anyone rudely asks, "Who farted? Did you fart?" The polite thing to do is to always say, "Of course not, not me, must have been that man with the umbrella."

If you notice a fart and don't want to call attention to it, you could politely say something like, "Oh, it's stuffy in here. I'm getting a headache. Let's open a window." Now I know your interest in honesty and straightforwardness may cringe at these suggestions. Some will even say we are not being truthful when we deny our own emissions or the emissions of others, but remember, you, who are so interested in being polite, also recognize that most manners are really small lies. When we are asked, "Do you like my new Spandex shorts," or "How do you like my new boyfriend," most of us are polite and say "Nice," or "He's just lovely," even if the former makes our friend look like he's wearing spray paint or the later is a Hollywood fashion queen into combat boots and Vanity Fair magazine. Whether guided by formal rules of etiquette or just navigating by the seat of your pants, being polite instead of radically honest saves many of us.

And speaking of seats, now is as good a time as any to comment on the slow but insidious transformation taking place with the theater seats of America. If you are troubled by loud farts, you ought to be doubly troubled by this outrageous decadence. At one time you could go to the theater and sit on a nice spring and fabric cushion. A velvet or tapestry cover would breathe as you shifted your weight, and most importantly, it absorbed farts.

In a theater that seats about a thousand, there are bound to be about one hundred farts every fifteen minutes or so. That's quite a few little Phantoms of the Opera sent floating into the atmosphere. Over the course of a three act play, opera or concert, a lot can be digested. All that methane, from an audience that just ate a rich meal, had many potent drinks or is nervous about being with the one they're with, escapes into a room. Those old fabric seats, however, had the advantage of absorbing all that gas and releasing it slowly enough so our collected noses hardly noticed a whiff. The newer seats of plastic and non-absorbent fibers create a surface that lets the farts slide right into the atmosphere. Their nonabsorbent surface probably doesn't cushion the sound as well. As soon as a fart is rent, it is spent. The willing suspension of disbelief is hardly possible in an atmosphere of squeaks, sputters and odors.

It seems, too, that these modern plastic seats are not just in theaters; you find them on the bus, at the bingo hall, in bars, in classrooms, all over. I guess it's just another sign of what happens when we try to offer everyone the same standard product: we end up with everyone getting something inferior. Isn't it odd, how the consideration of the simple fart leads us to realize one of the flaws in liberal democracy? Because we are animals, we fart, and because we fart we realize human nature cannot be perfected through material means alone. The fart speaks to us a deep truth about our mortality and limitations. The low, bass voice of our guts has a language all its own, and its revelations are essential to an understanding of the human predicament. Consideration of the lowly fart points us to the portals of the spirit.

Any consideration of the fart in regard to our existential predicament leads naturally to a consideration of the fart in human history. Why, even prehistory ought not to be passed over lightly. For example, while we don't know if insects fart like humans, because they lack soft parts, some biologists argue that if it weren't for the methane that termites add to the atmosphere, the percentage of oxygen would be too great to support life as we know it. Then there are all the cows and gorillas and the other animals who ingest great quantities of vegetation and emit a veritable symphonic rumble in the forests and jungles at night to add to what we breathe. Some say the farting of elephants can be heard for miles. Is this not a type of air pollution that rivals the pollution from our cars and trucks choking city streets?

The above observations are not just the grumblings of an old man. An English newspaper, The Scotsman reports in its December 20th, 2001 issue that scientists in New Zealand have concluded that the biggest cause of global warming is not the burning of coal or oil, but in fact the farts of cows and sheep. The methane released by New Zealand's 45 million sheep and 8 million cattle accounts for 44% of domestically produced greenhouse gasses. It is assumed that gasses in turn contribute to global warming. New Zealand has the the world's highest per capita methane production, amounting to six times the global average.

Many people do not dwell on the damage farts can do, but every once in a while there is shocking evidence. In a recent article by Habegger and O'Reilly in the Chicago Tribune for Sunday, March 3rd, 1991, they discuss the damage done to artworks in England. They write, "Scientists at the University of East Anglia give two major culprits in the deterioration of paintings, photographs and other works of art: fumes from the wet wool clothing worn by visitors to museums and galleries on rainy days and gas from flatulent art lovers. Do your part for the ages: Stay dry and avoid gas-producing food." One of the authors of the study, Peter Brimblecombe, a specialist in atmospheric chemistry, told the reporters, "If people have to go to galleries and museums, they should wear no clothes and control themselves."

It is not just art museums that are worried about farts. We can see the same preoccupation coming out of art schools. The F Newsmagazine of the School of the Art Institute of

Chicago runs a regular column entitled "Who Farted?" It is billed as a look at who's passing gas in the art community. In it we read quotes and comments by known and unknown artists. I assume the point of all this is to deplete even more of the earth's protective ozone layer. I wonder if the editors know of the San Francisco based writer Richard Rodriques. He described the air above Mexico City as "brown, fungal, farted." I have seen Wicker Park galleries in Chicago where the art on the walls could be described the same way. Could this be the naked truth about modern art? It is ironic too that the only thing that separates "art" from "fart" is the sixth letter in the alphabet. But I digress; let me catch my wind and resume the course I originally set.

To talk about the fart in human history is often to talk about assholes. As far back as St. Augustine's City of God, we can read about people who could talk with their assholes. Could we be witnessing in our political oratory today a return of this phenomenon? Needless to say, if someone is going to speak with his asshole, he will need a source of breath. This is where the fart takes on a new fluency. The ability to control the fart, its pressure, length, etc., are indispensable in training the asshole to speak. I remember as a girl reading a novel in which one of the characters talked with his asshole. The problem was he could not control it. Things soon got out of hand. To mix a metaphor, he bit off more than he could chew. He ended up having violent arguments with his other end. They were so loud, he was eventually thrown out of his apartment and left to carry on the best he could in the streets. These were the days before Late Night with David Letterman, where he could probably have found employment, and the country would be richer for his talent.

On a higher note, we should also remember that in days past, the term for poetic inspiration, the type of inspiration I hope guides my essay, was nothing other than "Divine Afflatus." Is this how God talks to man? Although this term is much abused now and often considered an insult rather than a compliment, the divine afflatus has been credited with much that is great in arts and letters. Consider the French writer Jean Genet. He writes of smelling his own farts in jail. What better picture could we have of the self-centered, self-contained artists? Or consider Dante. Being much inspired while writing the Divine Comedy, Dante has one of the devils at the end of Canto 21 in "The Inferno" use his abilities to fart. This allows the visitors of hell to pass into a lower region. In the freely translated words of the bard, as they approached the bridge, "To announce we were going to pass, he made a trumpet of his ass."

In our time, the derivative monsters and devils of Stephen King reflect back to this moment in Dante. In King's book, It, there is also such a use of the announcing fart. Not to be outdone, the Devil may even have the last word in all this bantering. George Bernard Shaw has him remark in his play, Don Juan in Hell, that "flatulent philosophers" are not to be trusted.

The English poet Samuel Butler likewise considered the fart a source of poetic inspiration in his satire on Puritanism, a long mock-heroic poem called Hudibras. Here we find the inspiring lines:

> He would an elegy compose
> On maggots squeez'd out his nose:
> In lyric numbers write an ode on
> His mistress, eating a black-pudden:
> And, when imprison'd air escap'ed her,

It puft him up with poetic rapture.

Perhaps it is with the concept of the divine afflatus that we can pass from Augustine to Martin Luther. Who can forget Luther's famous remark, "If I fart in Wittenberg, maybe they'll hear me in Rome." It may be that those who see this statement as direct insight into the German soul, look at things from the wrong side up. Nevertheless, there seems to be something about German culture that brings out what is fundamental in us. Of course, farting was not the only preoccupation Luther had. He also had tight bowels. Maybe it is revisionist history, but some say if they had Ex-Lax then, we might not have had the Protestant Reformation! And if Max Weber is right, no Protestant Reformation, means no capitalism. No capitalism, means no modern world as we know it. It reminds one of that old song, "For the Want of a Nail." The fart is woven into the very fabric of our modern, urban, industrial civilization. The fart is venture capitalism, corporate takeovers, pork futures. To think of a world without farts is to think of a world without money. Such thinking would no doubt please Ezra Pound, who wrote in Canto XIV of the "vice-crusaders, farting through silk, waving the Christian symbols..."

The first documented use of the word, "fart," in English is given as 1250 by The Oxford English Dictionary. In 1386 Chaucer used it in his "Miller's Tale," where he wrote, "He was somdel squaymous Of farting." Chaucer then goes on to relate an incident that ends in tragedy. Attempting to play a cruel joke on poor Absolon, Nicholas decides to fart in Absolon's face. In Chaucer's words:

> Speke swete bird, I n'ot wher thou art.
> This Nicholas anon let fleen a fart,
> As gret as it had ben a thonder dint,
> That with the stroke he was wel nie yblint:

Taken aback by this blast, Absolon applies a hot poker to Nicholas' ass. This leads to much consternation among all involved. Here it seems Nicholas bit off more than Absolon could chew.

There is also another incident in Chaucer's, The Summoner's Tale, involving a fart. Here we give Chaucer's in translation. The English is modern, but the fart is the same as it ever was.

"Ha!" thought the friar. "Here lies good luck for me!"

And quickly thrust his hand below the rift,
And full of hope that he would find his gift.
And when the sick man felt this greedy friar
Groping about, all eager with desire,
Into the friar's hand he let a fart.
No cart-horse, tugging strongly at his cart,
Could ever let a fart that louder sounded.

Since Chaucer's time, the word, "fart," has been a favorite of English satirical writing. Ben Johnson and others used it freely, but it is with the French that a taste for farting and its literary application developed to perfection.

For this evidence, we can look to none other than the French essayist Montaigne. Although Montaigne had trouble with his kidneys rather than his bowels, in chapter XII of his Essays, "Apology for Raimond Sebond," Montaigne writes, "Metrocles broke wind a little carelessly while disputing in the presence of his school and hid himself in his house for shame, until Crates came to visit him, and, adding to his consolation and arguments the example of his own freedom, starting to break wind in rivalry with him, relieved him of that scruple; and besides, drew him to his own Stoical sect, which was freer, from the more polite Peripatetics, whom he had followed till then." The fart from that moment on was aligned with freedom and social revolution. Since the days of ancient Greece, the fart has been the enemy of tyrants and dictators everywhere.

We moderns think we are something special when we release a film called F.A.R.T, The Movie on CD and video tape in 2002. How little do we know ourselves or the fart. Let Peter Dronke teach us another lesson in humility. In his collection of essays, Verse with Prose from Petronius to Dante (Harvard University Press), Dronke show us that in classical times many authors were aware of the fart's potential to invoke laughter and deflate authority. In a reference to Seneca's satire, The Play About Claudius' Death, Seneca use the fart to poke fun at the Roman emperor and tyrant, Claudius. To quote Dronke, "Claudius in the Ludus is first present with rude humor: his 'famous last words" are a fart accompanied by the cry "Oh dear, I think I've shit myself!" (vae me, puto, concacavi me!). His speech defect and limp are also mocked."

Farts accompany tyrants wherever they go. A short hop from Greece to France to Germany can make this point. According to Hitler's architect, Albert Speer, in his book Inside the Third Reich, Hitler suffered greatly from excessive gas in the digestive tract. Besides his regular doctor, Karl Brandt, Hitler consulted and took the advice of Dr. Theodore Morell, who, in his own book, describes the treatment he gave Hitler. According to Speer, Hitler "often interrupted a conference because of his gastric pains and withdrew for half an hour or more, or did not return at all. He also suffered...from excessive gas...." It is ironic to think that the great orator, Hitler, also projected greatness from the nether regions. Perhaps it is simply the case that great oration and great flatulence go hand in hand, or is it better to say tongue-in-cheek?

This little aside to Germany taken in stride, let us return to France and the examples she offers. Besides Montaigne, the French also gave us Joseph Pujol, better known as "Le petomane." He was born in Marseilles in 1857 and had the remarkable ability of controlling the muscles in his anus and stomach. He could ingest through his anus great quantities of water and air and then release them under his own control. Eventually, with such a talent, he devised a music hall act where he would imitate all kinds of farts such as the timid fart, the hearty miller's fart, the fart of the bride on her wedding night, etc. He could even play popular tunes with the help of an ocarina attached to a tube which he inserted in his rectum offstage. It is reported he could let a fart that lasted a full ten seconds. Some even say he could blow out candles and stage footlights with the force of his wind. With this talent he became immensely wealthy and popular. Jealousy of such wealth may be why recently a British man built a giant fart machine on the English cost and aimed it at France.

In their biography, Le Petomane, by Jean Nohain and F. Caradec, published by Bell Publishing Company, New York City, we learn that Le Petomane only farted in the best of places, and for considerable money. As a star of the famous Moulin Rouge in Paris from 1892 to 1914, he drew gates of 20,000 francs, while Sara Bernhardt only managed 8,000 francs.

Pujol died in 1945 at the age of 88. If anyone has ever worked their way from the bottom up, surely he did. As of today, neither the French, nor anyone else, has resurrected this example of civilization for stage or screen. Perhaps it is for the best. How are you going to keep them down on the farm after they've heard Pujol?

Of course when it comes to French farts, probably the most famous was the one cut by Pantagruel. We may read about this exploit in *The Histories of Gargantua and Pantagruel* by François Rabelais. Chapter twenty-seven of Book II, in the J. M. Cohen translation, reads: "...with the fart he blew, the earth trembled for twenty-seven miles round, and with the fetid air of it he engendered more than fifty-three thousand little men, misshapen dwarfs; and with a poop, which he made, he engendered as many little bowed women, such as you see in various places, and who grow, except downwards like cows' tails, or in circumference, like Limousin turnips. "'What now,' exclaimed Panurge. 'Are your farts so fruitful? By God, here are fine clumpish men, fine stinking women. Only let them be married together, and they'll breed horseflies.' So Pantagruel did, and called them pygmies."

Could there be a fart more powerful than Pantagruel's? For an answer to this question we must turn to Native American mythology. Dr. Wendall Wilson, a Jungian enthusiast, showed me an article by Paul Radin on the exploits of the Trickster in North American Indian societies.

Here we can read about the adventure of the Winnebago trickster-hero, Wakdjunkaga.

Radin writes, "So he takes the bulb and chews it to find that he does not defecate but only breaks wind. This expulsion of gas increases in intensity progressively. He sits on a log, but is propelled into the air....he pulls up trees to which he clings, by their roots. In his helplessness he has the inhabitants of a village pile all their possessions upon him....And so now the whole world is on Wakdjunkaga's back. With a terrific expulsion of gas he scatters the people and all their possessions to the four quarters of the earth."

I doubt if there ever has been or will be a fart to match that one by Wakdjunkaga. Neil Simon suggests in his play, Biloxi Blues, that one of the soldiers could pass such gas that it would blow up the world, but this is in the context of a barracks discussion of what one would do with their last week on earth. In this case, the fart is introduced as a destructive element. Pantagruel's and Wakdjunkaga's farts are just the opposite; they are fruitful and resonate with such implications for history and cultural evolution! Then again, if you had a bad day and are on a crowded elevator, an ordinary fart let by that unsavory type way in the back may seem as loud and pregnant as the fart that ended the world.

Many poets and philosophers have given their attention to the fart. Buried deep in the bowels of Hegel's Phenomenology of Spirit is a pointed but obscure reference to it. After discussing the differences between the universal and individual consciousness from the point of view of utility, Hegel writes, "The beyond ... hovers over the corpse of the vanished independence of real being ... merely as the exhalation of a stale gas, of the vacuous Etre suprême." Ah, Hegel, what a way with words--spoken like a true German.

If the translation of Rainer Maria Rilke by Stephen Mitchell is correct, even that poet fell prey to the fundamental German interest in ends as opposed to beginnings. Mitchell translates the phrase, "*die warm in sei hineinvomieren, und blasende Gesäße, die ihnen Gefallen tun*," from The Notebooks of Malte Laurids Brigge, as "and faces that warmly vomit onto them, and windy buttocks that offer them satisfaction." What kind of satisfaction could those windy buttocks offer, I wonder? Does this have anything to do with the fact Germans often put the engines in the back of their cars or are overly fond of food resembling fecal matter, like sausages?

When I was in high school, I had to read J. D. Salinger's Catcher in the Rye. Salinger writes: "All of a sudden this guy sitting in the row in front of me, Edgar Marsalla, laid this terrific fart. It was a very crude thing to do, in chapel and all...." Of course a loud fart in church by definition seems funny, but what interests me in this description is the use of the phrase "laid this terrific fart." The expression, "to lay a fart," now seems outdated. Most people I know use the expression, "to cut a fart," as in the question, "Who cut a fart?" I think this is more popular than "laid a fart," because it makes reference to the euphemism, "To cut the cheese," where the relationship between the odor of certain cheeses and farts no doubt is firmly established in the popular mind. This reference to cheese notwithstanding, perhaps the expression, "to lay a fart," is related to the idea of laying an egg. The feel of a fart and the feel of an egg, as they leave their respective bodies, may be similar.

Just recently, the English poet Philip Larkin made reference to the fart. He composed these lines in a poem called, "The Card-Players."

Dirk deals the cards. Wet century-wide trees
Clash in surrounding starlessness above
This lamplit cave, where Jan turns back and farts,
Gobs at the gate, and hits the queen of hearts.

Larkin writes in another of his poems, "Posterity" about a man assigned to write the biography of a poet. The biographer is seated in his "air-conditioned cell" of the library and worries, "I'm stuck with this old fart at least a year..." Andrew Motion thinks this line is predictive of Larkin's own opinion of those who will one day write his biography.

In a story Larkin and his friend Kingsley Amis wrote when they were young men, Larkin displays his gift for apt metaphor. The story was called, "The Tale of the Jolly Prince and the Distempered Ghost," and was a saga about a farting medieval ghost. The text of this saga seems to be lost, but a fragment remains: "and then the ghost made a fart like the breaking of an apple branch under the weight of good fruit." Isn't that the most delightful of images? Just imagine what the rest of the text must have contained! And to think this was all the work of a ghost. Ghost farts are a new area to explore. Unfortunately, this essay must limit itself to the human fart. Farts from beyond the grave must remain another subject for another day.

Not to be outdone, on the other side of the ocean, the American poet John Ashbery, writing in his book, *Flow Chart*, remarked, "Excuse me while I fart. There, that's better. I actually feel relieved." Poets can be so polite, even if there verse is free.

Sometimes entire works of poetry are dedicated to the fart. The Chicago poet Shérée Anne Slaughter has written a poem called, "May the Fart Be With You," the best lines of which are:

> "When the boss is getting all on your case
> That's right, fart, he'll get out of your face."

Turning from poetry to prose, in a 1988 novel, Brothers in Arms, by Michael Carson, a book which a New York Times reviewer described as, "Cheeky, humorous...a young man's coming-of-age story with a twist...a book whose strength is ribald realism," we read of two incidents involving the fart. The book's hero, Benson, has returned to his old school after a year away and is forced to read his essay on Hamlet to the class. "That Hamlet does not see this, does not appreciate the Ghost, is probably a temptation of the Devil, says much for his woeful ignorance of the tenets of the Catholic Church. Somebody farted." Undaunted, he continues reading to the growing laughter in the classroom. There is nothing like a fart to add humor to the most serious situation. We must wonder also if the young man who interrupted the reading anguished over, to fart or not to fart, that is the question.

The second incident occurs later in the book when the same young man is picked up by an older man, and the two of them return to the older man's apartment to have sex. As Benson allows the older man to fellate him, "He moaned and listened to Andy's muffled moans and the fart-like slurps he was making with his embrace." This is the first time I know of in English literature that the metaphor of the fart is used to describe oral sex. Perhaps Publishers Weekly is right when they say the author has "A wicked eye for detail and an obvious familiarity with the milieu."

In a much praised book, Martin and John, by Dale Peck, the fart introduces us to the tragic perspective of AIDS and death. Peck writes, "I was almost ready to help him out of the tub, when a long fart bubbled out of the water, filling the bathroom with sound and smell. Didn't know you still had it in you, I said without turning, and I washed the shaving cream off my face." Peck then goes on to meditate on the passing of life and a relationship. In his prose, the fart become a key by which the author opens the doors of reflection. *Sic transit gloria mundi.*

The fart and sex come together in a more usual way in an erotic poem called "Haiku: Safe Sex," by Zero Hopeloff. It is published in the magazine *Quarterly*, #22, Summer 1992, by Vintage books. I like this poem. It has a Zen quality about it that opens new frontiers of reflection on the dialectics of relationships. It reads:

> The slub of your tongue
> flush against my loosened seam --
> I will try not to fart.

I assume the whole point of the poem is to stop trying. Just let it go. Relax! Let nature flow through. The harder you try, the less powerful you are. I can see the teeth gritting in the line, "I will try not to fart." And then the release, the freedom that comes with the realization we are accepted in love, accepted by our lover. Man, such sensibility in only three lines.

But do these three lines compare with lines written by the master of haiku, the Japanese poet, Kobayashi Issa? In a unique translation of a fart poem to English, David G. Lanoue convinces me Issa is the master. You decide.

blown
away
by
the
horse's
fart
firefly

Certainly other examples of poetry from the history of English literature could be cited. How many of us can recall the little verse we learned in childhood about the glory and wonder of beans? "Beans, beans, the musical fruit, the more you eat, the more you toot, the more you toot, the better you feel, so let's have beans at every meal." There is also a variation that goes, "Beans, beans, good for the heart, the more you eat the more you..." You get the point.

Little did we know as children about the power and symbolism of beans. If we had read, then, The White Goddess by Robert Graves, we would have known that beans were filled with wondrous powers and ought not be mocked. Graves tells us in his book that the Pythagorean mystics were bound by a strong taboo against eating beans. To eat beans was to eat one's parents' heads. This superstition was similar to the views held by the Platonists. They excluded beans on the rationalistic ground that they caused flatulence. Life, they argued, was breath, and to break wind after eating beans was proof one had eaten a living soul. What would these philosophers have made of a product like Beano, a product that prevents farts? If one ate beans with Beano, would that be a kind of spiritual abortion? Maybe this is an example of the fart cutting both ways.

Rugby songs for adults, with their catchy words and tunes, are often as popular as those little songs about beans we sang in childhood. Long famous for their sexual references, rugby songs have been known also to include references to the fart. One of my fondest memories of being a young woman is sitting on a mountain in Wales drinking hard cider with my English friends and singing verses from such songs. It seemed as if you could see all of England from that vantage point and that our voices would be broadcast around the globe. For those interested, a fine book called, Why Was He Born So Beautiful and Other Rugby Songs, by Sphere Books, Great Britain, 1967, with a preface by Michael Green, offers many examples of such songs. I modestly present two here; the first is a couplet from, "The Ball of Kerrymuir" that has the memorable lines,

> The chimney sweep he was there,
> They had to throw him out,
> For every time he passed his wind
> The room was filled with soot.

The second is from a little song called, "Life Presents a Dismal Picture."

> Even now the baby's started
> Having epileptic fits,
> Every time it coughs it spews
> Every time it farts it shits.

Finally, what would any song feast be like without a limerick? We used to especially enjoy the following:

> There was a young poet named Martin,
> Whose life was very Spartan
> For lunch he'd eat greens,
> For supper baked beans,
> Then look for a field to fart in.

Even though the fart is so important in human history, one soon discovers there are few good books or essays totally devoted to it. The above book makes only slight reference to what is the major concern of this essay. After reviewing the literature, I recommend the following as more dedicated. Dan Sabbath and Mandel Hall's book, End Product, is a treasure of fecal and gaseous anecdotes. Perhaps the classic piece about the fart and its effects in English literature is the work, 1601, Conversations as it was by the social fireside in the time of the Tudors, by Mark Twain.

In this elegant essay, Twain relates how a discussion around a fire eventually comes to the question of who farted in the presence of the Queen. "In ye heat of ye talk it befel yt one did breake wind, yielding an exceding mightie and distresfull stink, whereat all did laugh full sore..." Sr. Walter Raleigh finally admits, "Most gracious magisty, 'twas I that did it, but indeed it was so poor and frail a note, compared with such as I am wont to furnish, yt in sooth I was ashamed to call the weakling mine...then delivered he himself of such a godless and rockshivering blast it did come so dense and full a stink that that which went before did seem a poor and trifling thing beside it." Twain knew that in a democracy, one need not bow before any man or woman, and if we do, what better comment to make about parasitical royalty than while bowing, to fart.

In 1973, "and Books" of South Bend, Indiana, published a pamphlet by Cannum called, On Farts. This illustrated booklet has sections on the types and degrees of fart odors and an especially helpful section on the atmospheric spreading effects of farts. The author also has suggestions for dealing with farts in bed. Her remedy for dealing with farts trapped under blankets--using the leg to create an escape tunnel--should be more widely known.

Just in time for the Holiday Season, Bastien Publications, Des Plaines, Il., has come out with what they call "The Ideal

Stocking Stuffer for Farters." It is a paper titled *Farters News.* When you purchase the paper you receive free a lifetime membership card for the person of your choice to Farters Anonymous. In light of the thesis of my essay, this may seem a bit redundant, since I do argue most farters are anonymous or should aim to be so, but nevertheless both items can be obtained for the small sum of only $9.95.

To bring our references of the fart up to date, I am compelled to add a report about the Conference on College Composition and Communication which took place at Chicago's Palmer House Hotel in March 1990. Many English teachers go to these conferences to get out of their small university towns and have a gas in the big city, but one can also learn something about the direction the winds of academia are blowing by watching and listening. According to the Chicago poetry newsletter, Letter eX, the poet X. J. Kennedy read a poem at a conference session called "Ode" in which he addressed his asshole. One section of the poem dealt with what he called, "The Cave of the Winds." It is good to hear the conference was not fart free.

The report about the Conference on College Composition and Communication reminded me of a joke I had heard earlier. Why don't little girls fart? Because they don't get assholes till they're married. Could this be the reason why some poets don't fart either? They only become assholes when they become critics.

Little girls and women don't get off so easily elsewhere. One commentator, the outrageous comedian Gallagher, whose shows are legendary for the physical abuse he heaps upon his audience, remarked recently on his cable TV special, "Women can't keep a secret, but they can hold a fart. So, if you ever want to tell a women a secret, whisper in their ass."

In order to increase the body of serious literature on the fart, I composed a short poem on the subject of farting. It is inspired by Montaigne's insightful anecdote and its intellectual consequence. I include it at this point in my essay for your enjoyment.

Philosophy

Our science shows the thing apart,
the thing entire is grasped by art.

But how to live, by mind or heart --
that is the same for us as Metrocles,
who was converted by a fart.

This mention of philosophy makes me remember that, while I was in college, I had a philosophy class in which we seriously considered for a time why it is that we have the social convention of coughing to get someone's attention, but not farting. Imagine what kind of society it would be if we were to come into a room, and it was accepted that we could announce our presence by a fart? Certainly this would be a more just society, and one that would have probably saved the life of an unfortunate Argentinean doctor.

We live, however, in a different world than the one imagined in a philosophy class. It is a world that is still deficient in its anal vocabulary. Just think of all the expressions, like, "to clear one's throat," that relate to expulsion of air from the mouth. There is nothing to compare to these expression for the nether regions. Of course, we can say "juicy fart" or "smelly fart" or "old fart," but there are many more anal phenomenon and sensations that lack a proper diction. Is an "atomic fart", which is fifty percent fallout, accurately described?

Consider for a moment that unique sensation of having a turd stuck in your asshole. Or maybe it's a fart that won't escape. Nevertheless, our language is deficient in that it lacks a word for this particular sensation. We can't use the expression, "Stuck up," because that already relates to another type of deficiency. Perhaps someone with more talent than I will dedicate their life to the fundamental problem of increasing our anal vocabulary.

Before they do that, however, a note of caution. The expression "old fart" ought to be used with care. Recently, a District of Columbia judge awarded a 54-year-old man $400.000.00 in damages in his age-discrimination lawsuit against his former employer. According to the plaintiff, his supervisor continually made references to his age, including addressing him as an "old fart." It looks like we are going have to put our heads together and come up with some better terms. Failing that, be prepared to pay dearly for your insults.

Maybe that should be the calling of Larry Kramer, the New York playwright. The last time I read an article by him in the Chicago newspaper, Windy City Times, his writing was filled with words like "shithead," "fuckhead," etc. His subtext was such a torrential rain of invectives using anal and genital references as to convince anyone that the man loathed all bodily excretion. He never once used the word, "fart," however.

Perhaps Kramer should take a lesson from Florence King. In her new book, Lump It or Leave It, she harkens back to Rabelais and is creative enough to refer to children as "fartlings." Maybe if we call it to Kramer's attention, he can turn his talents to exploring the fundamental area of our anatomy and help create a proper diction to celebrate the fart.

Until then, all I have to offer are the few verses above. They are as inspired as I can make them, on a windy afternoon in August, contemplating my bowl of cabbage and beans. I hope they point to the role of the fart in the study of metaphysics and teach us the unique, human lesson of the fart: we learn how to live from our minds as well as our bodies. Pray that such knowledge is never lost.

If we cannot learn this lesson, than maybe we can at least be polite. To make this point I rely on an example from the

Chicago newspaper, Windy City Times. In a penetrating article on the difference between a "Daddy" and a "Dad" (a title much debated in the gay community and sometime modified by the adjective "sugar"), the columnist "G" writes, "Dad never understood that farting was noxious and impolite....he would galumph across the living room in front of guests and relatives, erupting like a string of underwater volcanoes. The resulting jetstream would invariably cause you to flee outdoors. Daddy, on the other hand, never farts out loud. He is a well-disciplined slow leaker, careful never to draw attention to his gentle zephyrs. Not even a Mexican combination platter perturbs his gastronomical sang froid." Men and women everywhere should heed this sound advice and act accordingly.

Advice also could be offered to those who listen to their personal stereos while they work out at gyms and health clubs. Beyond the fact that farts can probably carry germs, the invention and distribution of the personal stereo with earphones has created a unique problem for farters. Those who have used this device know the earphones mask our hearing. What seems to be a modest singing along with the music often ends up being a loud nuisance for our neighbors.

Imagine what this means, when listening to our personal stereo, for the decision to pass a fart in the gym while jogging or using an exercise bike. We must ask ourselves, even it we don't hear its thunder, whether or not our fart will be an intrusion on our neighbor using the next treadmill or stair climber. After all, they might not be listening to their stereo full blast and resent being interrupted by our sputterings.

As anyone knows who has used a diabolical exercise machine, working out on them does have a tendency to massage our lower tract and loosen what otherwise might stay in place until we are in a more private location. Realizing these difficulties, a friend of mine who works out regularly at the gym has developed a simple procedure that avoids much embarrassment.

When he notices the pressure building, he removes one of his earphones in a discreet manner and does what he calls a "test release." If he hears nothing behind him, the earphone goes back on, the volume is cranked up, the jogging continues and he lets them rip. And rip they will, as we have through the pages of this little tract. Now that I am approaching the end of my essay, I regret that a few questions still remain unanswered. The attentive reader realizes I only considered the question of farts among mammals. Other questions could now be entertained. For example, do plants fart, and what about birds or fish, do they also fart?

If we apply St. Thomas Aquinas' three part analogy to the issue of farts among plants, animals and mankind, we can come to a startling conclusion. Aquinas argued plants have their mouths, that is to say their roots, in the earth. This is how they suck up nourishment. At the other end, the leaves of a plant, their anus, are waving in the wind. This is how they dispose of waste.

The byproducts of photosynthesis are oxygen and water. The expulsion of oxygen by the leaves of a plant could be considered a plant fart, for it is gas escaping into the atmosphere. There are no muscles to control this expulsion, however, and for this reason the emission of gas is gradual. I know of no plant that expels gas in such a manner as to wake the sleeping with an explosive roar, as human farts are known to do.

The good saint also noted that mammals and fish have their mouths and anus on the same leave, that is, one could draw a horizontal line from mouth to anus. It is only in human beings that the mouth is above the anus. This is a complete reversal of the plant's mouth-anus relationship. Such a reversal points to a hierarchy in creation that demonstrates the significance of language in human beings and their naturally authority and superiority over plants and animals.

As to the question of fish farts, for various and complex reasons involving diet and anatomy, and the necessity of a swim bladder filled with gas in some species of fish, it remains difficult to say whether or not all fish dispose of intestinal gas in a farting manner. Nevertheless, after much handwringing and back and forth arguments, it can now be said with certainty that some fish do fart, at least that is what Francesca Gould claims in her book "Why Fish Fart & Other Useless or Gross Information About the World."

"(The)bubbles coming from the backside of a cod are not technically farts but those near a herring's are ...The escaping air emits a high-pitched sound that scientists think is used to communicate with other herrings at night. No other fish can detect the noise of their emissions: The herring farts are silent."

Can the same can be said in regard to the question of bird farts, a fart on the wing so to speak? We know so very little through observation that an answer to the question of bird farts remains up in the air.

Like the subject of fish farts and birdn farts, pussy farts are also relatively new to the literature on farts. Furthermore, like fish farts, pussy farts are considered by many to be a controversial subject. Pussy farts are also for purposes of this essay a misnomer. If by "pussy farts" we mean "cat or feline farts," then the experience of pet owners forces us to conclude that yes, cats like dogs, do indeed fart. But that is not what most people mean by "pussy farts." In fact they are referring to some type of vaginal, gaseous emission. By this definition, we must exclude pussy farts from the category of real farts. Real farts and the farts discussed in this essay are not virginal emission but emissions from the anus. Nevertheless, the topic of pussy farts has made its way to the internet and the world wide web. The web page "http://www.rocketpack.org/raymicunt_trumpet_music.html"

has an interesting discussion of this topic. "So, I've been asking around about pussy farting. About queefs. I've been searching high and low for hard facts. And nothing. I did come across a website boasting of Girls who like to smell Farts and eat Pussy Cheese. Not exactly helpful to my cause. What I have found is, there are plenty of uneducated people out there. Specifically Men." Our source continues, "I don't understand how men can be disgusted by a pussy fart, which in reality is not even a fart. It's this polite little sound that comes out of a twat. It's more of a... Thank you for humping me and thrusting all that air inside. And then comes this cute little Whooooosh of air. Men don't have any right to be all grossed out and make us ladies embarrassed about it. It's not even our fault. I'm certain any orifice would make a sound if you shoved something in it over and over and over again, real fast and hard.

Fact: Pussy farts don't even smell. If they did they'd smell like candy or roses or peaches. There is no chance a queef would ever smell like hot garbage or rotting egg salad. Ew. A pussy fart is air only. Air smells like nothing. So there you go.

Fact: Pussy farting is fun. You think all girls ever did at slumber parties was eat popcorn and talk about stupid boys? Fuck no. We get down on our hands and knees, squeeze our poons real tight and Whooooooooosh ourselves across the floor. Or we lie on our backs and put our legs in the air as if we were doing that bicycle exercise, suck in our stomachs a bit then drop our legs real fast. This helps make a nice sharp queef. Something to be proud of. Definitely. Some girls know their shit when it comes to serious queefing, emitting blast after blast with ease. It sounds easy, but takes skill. Some say it's easier if you're loose. Others claim it's the control of your PC muscle that helps. Regardless, it is entirely possible, sometimes spontaneous and can be embarrassing if you whoooosh out of context. But it's funny, so don't get all sad about it and never call that guy/girl again for frapping your poon in their face. Go out with style. You'll give 'em another and they'll like it."

So far, our conclusion must be that only land animals truly fart. The human fart unites us with a select species of animals. Add to that union the cultural and social creations surrounding the fart in human societies, and it is evident mankind is separated even farther from the animal and plant kingdoms. The human fart remains a unique phenomenon worthy of many an essay.

The ancient Greeks knew all too well the truth about farts. Once again, the old wisdom reminds us how little we have changed over the centuries. The ancients knew the terrible implications of a philosophy that denies our human nature. They also knew how to take learning lightly and poke fun at a wisdom that pretends to be serious. Aristophanes does this well in The Clouds. There he chides both students and teachers. He does so by employing the simple fart. One of Socrates' students, so impressed with his master's knowledge, a knowledge that includes insight on how a gnat hums, inadvertently displays the triviality of much science when he argues, "The entrails of the gnat is small: and through this narrow pipe the wind rushes with violence straight toward the tail; there, close against the pipe, the hollow rump receives the wind, and whistles to the blast."

Socrates is likewise the butt of a joke when he discusses the origins of thunder. Aristophanes has him say, "Shalt thou then a sound so loud and profound from thy belly diminutive send, and shall not the high and infinite Sky go thundering on without end? For both, you will find, on an impulse of wind and similar causes depend." Happy those who know themselves. The fart spoke about human truths for the ancient Greeks. Their example motivates me to consider dashing off a short correction to an otherwise sound advice column read by many in our local newspaper. But now I have second thoughts. If I send this essay as a letter, will the editor think I am too windy, or will my humble efforts be heard above the din and clamor of the belching crowd?

For too long, farts and farters have been discriminated against. Maybe my verse will help blow away some of that prejudice. I would like to break new wind on the subject, so to speak. If I can't add sweetness, maybe I can add another aroma. And if neither, I can at least offer my humble couplets, couplets which may be better appreciated the next time we consider the consequences of a plate of sauerkraut, beans, or for some, even cantaloupe and cucumbers.

From my own experience, I know one of the best ways to end discrimination against farters is to bring up our children with an appreciation and knowledge of farts. To this end, Kane/Miller Book Publishers deserves much credit. They now publish a children's book called, The Gas We Pass: The Story of Farts. This charmingly illustrated book by Shinta Cho was first published in Japan under the title *Onara (A Story of Farts)*. The English version is translated by Amanda Mayer Stinchecum and is printed in Singapore by Tien Wah Press Pte. Ltd.

This colorful book begins with the fact, "When an elephant farts, the farts are really big. Baaroomm." Then the author goes on to say, "People fart too." The illustration shows a boy standing in a bath followed by, "Bubbles rise...plip, plip, plip." This is an utterly delightful story even adults will enjoy. The more people that read and share this little book, the fewer people there will be to discriminate against those of us who are free with the gas we pass.

One of the best ways to prevent discrimination against farters is to share information. A reader who has come this far realizes the wealth of information about farts available if we just look. Indeed, there may be no end to the subject. Books, videos, CDs and articles about the fart abound. It is often difficult to keep an essay like mine up to date with all the new and exciting fart related products and research reported in the press and offered for sale. Only a few of the more recent ones can be discussed here. Coleman Barks has done us a great service by translating the work of the great mystic poet Jelaluddin Rumi. (C. Barks, trans., *The Essential Rumi*, Harper San Francisco, 1995, p.213) In the Persian poet's attempt to embrace both the body as well as the spirit, we would expect the fart would also appear in Rumi writings. So it does. In a poem titled "Human Honesty," Rumi describe an encounter between a mayor and a hypocrite. While camping in the open, the mayor lets fly an arrow at night that fells a howling wolf, "Who moaned and farted and died." The hypocrite thought it was his donkey instead and cried, "You've killed my donkey. I know my donkey's farts as well as I know water from wine." The mayor doubts this, claiming, "You impostor! In the rain, at midnight, at fifty yards, you can distinguish one fart from another!" The mayor goes on to say that the God-drunkenness of the hypocrite is also phony.

Rumi use the humble fart to teach us a great lesson here. So it is with this humble book, dear reader. The fart, like all things human, is best dealt with by moderation. I hope at the very least that one learns not to make outrageous claims for the power of farts or for using farts to identify your donkey on a rainy night.

In 1996 a new video by Noise On called American Flatulators hit the stores. Taking toilet humor to new depths, this pungent video parodies the popular TV show, "American Gladiators." The contestants have to match physical feats of the auditory and olfactory varieties. One commentator, who will have the final word and this video, said, "It stinks"

Ivory Tower Publishing Company, Inc. of Watertown, Massachusetts distributes The Fart Book, by Donald Wetzel. It is Item number 2131 in their list of books, which includes such titles as Eating Pussy: The Official Cat Cook Book, and The Absolutely Worst Fart Book. The Fart Book is an illustrated list of various farts in alphabetical order. Martin Riskin did the illustrations. One of the more interesting farts described is the Volkswagen Fart. The author writes, "Any good strong fart in a Volkswagen in the winter or anyhow with the windows closed is the deadly Volkswagen Fart. It can strangle people. While I am generally in favor of people farting whenever they have to fart, they really should try not to fart in a closed Volkswagen. It would be nice if this were one of the rare farts but it isn't."

An article in Men's Fitness magazine for August, 1996, by Michael Castleman, called "Gut Reactions" deals with all the glories and problems of the digestive tract. His discussion of the fart and it's social and biological implications is quite up to date. Castleman writes, "Flatulence, commonly known as farting, is the proverbial ill wind that blows no good. Studies show that the average adult passes gas from eight to twenty times every waking day--in other words, there's nothing unusual about tooting more than once an hour."

In a related matter concerning doctors and their advice, Doctor Andrew Weils's newsletter "Self Healing" often has news for those inclined to distrust the medical establishment. The October, 2001 issue deals with the question, "How can I prevent gas?" Doctor Weil writes, "What many people call excessive gas is actually normal: The average adult passes gas about 14 times a day." This is about one fart every two hours, quite a few more than what Castleman allows. Our reporter in Michigan replies, "I don't know about you, but I do much better than that! If this ratio is embarrassing to some people, the doctor recommends chewing a half-teaspoonful of fennel seeds. This is a natural ayurvedic remedy to prevent and treat gas.

Here is a metaphor by the poet W. S. Merwin from his book Asian Figures, New York: Atheneum, 1973, about a hapless minister. "His hundred days of sermons all gone in one fart." Likewise, this odd bit of knowledge is interesting. In Norwegian the word "motion" is fart. And then there are the jokes. Here is one that has been making the rounds of office e-mails. Once upon a time there was an elderly gentleman that was suffering from Alzheimer's. His wife of 40 years loved him very much, but she couldn't handle him any longer. He would wander about never knowing where he was or sometimes even who he was. She took him to a nursing home. At the nursing home, while the wife was filling out paperwork, a nurse had the gentleman sit in a chair. Slowly, the man started leaning to his left. The nurse ran over and put a pillow on his left side to prop him up. A few minutes later, he started leaning to his right. Again, the nurse ran over and put a pillow on his right side. Then he started leaning forward. Now, the nurse strapped him into the chair. About this time, his wife, having completed the paperwork, walked up to him and asked, "How do you like the place?" "I don't know." he said. "They won't let me fart."

Another story in the office e-mails concerns an old woman riding in an elevator in a very lavish New York City Building. At one stop, a young and beautiful woman gets into the elevator, radiating of expensive perfume. She turns to the old woman and says arrogantly, "Romance" by Ralph Lauren, $150 an ounce!" Then another young and beautiful woman gets on the elevator, and also very arrogantly turns to the old woman saying, "Chanel No. 5, $200 an ounce!" About three floors later, the old woman has reached her destination and is about to get off the elevator. Before she leaves, she looks both beautiful women in the eye, then bends over and farts and says, "Broccoli. 49 cents a pound."

Then there is the 2000 Survival Guide for Taking a Dump at Work. This essential office handbook encourages us to do the following: Memorize these definitions and pooping at work will become a pure pleasure.

ESCAPEE: A fart that slips out while taking a leak at the urinal or forcing poop in a stall. This is usually accompanied by a sudden wave of panic/embarrassment. This is similar to the hot flash you receive when passing an unseen police car & speeding. If you release an escapee, do not acknowledge it. Pretend it did not happen. If you are standing next to the farter at the urinal, pretend that you did not hear it. No one likes an escapee, it is uncomfortable for all involved. Making a joke or laughing makes both parties feel uneasy.

JAILBREAK (Used in conjunction with escapee): When forcing a poop, several farts slip out at a machine gun pace. This is usually a side effect of diarrhea or a hangover. If this should happen do not panic, remain in the stall until everyone has left the bathroom so to spare everyone the awkwardness of what just occurred.

Anatoly Liberman's article, "Gone with the Wind: More Thoughts on Medieval Farting," in Scandinavian Studies, is just brilliant in execution and scope. Liberman claims, "The tale of Einarr's fart at the banquet of King Haraldr in

'Morkinskinna' has received more attention than it deserves. Scholars claiming that the story explains Einarr's name, which could be translated to suggest a fart, fail to realize that the name preceded the fart, and that the name could denote the strength associated with strong farting in those days, a strength that an archer such as Einarr would have possessed. It is likely that the story was misconstrued over the ages, as it has many inconsistencies and fails to stand up to scrutiny like other tales of the era."

Also of interest is the new CD "Pull My Finger," available from HR Productions. This contribution to the literature of farts contains 99 tracks of flatulent sound effects. The CD is marketed as all natural and all disgusting. According to the packaging, "Pull My Finger" is the only flatulently funny collection of authentic fart sounds available on CD. All the farts are collected from actual gaseous emissions and none are fake or synthesized. You can even sing along with three musical "cuts." Included for your pleasure are such titles as, "James Brown Stains," "Packing Tape," "Jurassic Farts," and the ever popular, "Tuna Melt Madness."

Of course, what would our survey be without referencing local newspapers. Northern Exposure, a Michigan newspaper reports the following: Two Illinois women undergoing C-section births at Evanston Hospital on July 31, 2001, received the necrotizing fasciitis (flesh eating) bacteria when a surgeon passed gas in the operating room. The Chicago Tribune reported only that the bacteria were present in a surgeon's intestines and not in a throat culture, and probably entered the patients through the air, but Chicago Channel 5 News' experts carried out the logic and named flatus as the culprit. The two women, their babies, and the surgeon have been treated and are out of danger. Thank God! It is too bad these doctors did not know about the work of Buck Weimer of Pueblo, Colorado. According to a Denver Post story, Buck Weimer has sold his entire first run of airtight briefs called Under-Ease. According to the inventor, these briefs contain a charcoal filter lining that effectively prevents farts from escaping into the air. Now, not only must doctors scrub up before an operation, but they'd better buckle up as well.

Advances in medicine, however, are happening at breakneck speed. At the other end of the spectrum, knowing when a patient farts may help in his recovery. According to an article appearing in the "Weekly World News" for February 5th, 2002, the Japanese have invented a "toot detector." Dubbed "hohi kenshutsuki," it sells for about 200,00 yen and measures about the size of two boxes of facial tissues. The detector interfaces with the client by means of a vinyl tube that is secured to the inner thigh." Many doctors feel it is important to know if a postoperative patient is breaking wind. Farting is an indication that the digestive tract is returning to normal. This machine will allow doctors immediate feedback on such an important development.

What is good for the operating room may be good also for the front room. We may want to know about farts at home in order to avoid them. To this end, the January, 2002 issue of the catalog "Things You Never Knew Existed," carries an ad for a sale priced Motion Activated Fart Alarm at just $13.97. The catalog claims this alarm will make your home a "Fart Free Zone" in seconds. The alarm hangs easily on the wall with the supplied slots. Furthermore, the ad goes on to say that every home ought to have one of these alarms just like they have a smoke alarm. It uses four AAA batteries, which are not included.

Even into the twenty-first century, the fart continues to ground our ambitions to be anything other than human. According to a report, on December 5th, 2006, "An American Airlines flight was forced to make an emergency landing...after a passenger lit a match to disguise the scent of flatulence." The report continues, "The Dallas-bound flight was diverted to Nashville after several passengers reported smelling burning sulfur from the matches... All 99 passengers and five crew members were taken off and screened while the plane was searched and luggage was screened."

Then, the FBI questioned a passenger who admitted she struck the matches in an attempt to conceal a "body odor." She was just trying to be polite and disguise the odor of her fart with that of a burning match. So, we end where we began: What is polite and what is not? The flight took off again, but the woman was not allowed back on the plane. No one wanted her to strike again.

What is the future of farts? If farts on an airplane are a problem, what about farts on a spaceship? Orson Scott Card believes that in the future farts will be as frequent as farts in our own time. In his popular science fiction novel for young adults, Ender's Game, Card makes many references to farts.

The main character of the book, Ender Wiggin is referred to as the "little farthead." Another characters in the story is called a "gold-plated fart," and yet another is an "old farteater." Just imagine, for farts to be gold-plated or eaten, they must have a substance in the future that is far beyond their present gaseous nature. I can't wait for that time on some distant planet when someone says, "they cut a fart," and we have a slice of fart on our plate like a slice of smoked Edam cheese.

Meanwhile, back on earth, a new line of underwear employs chemical warfare technology to filter out the smell of its user's farts.The line of boxers and briefs, designed by Shreddies, "features a 'Zorflex' activated carbon back panel that absorbs all flatulence odours."

"Due to its highly porous nature, the odour vapours become trapped and neutralised by the cloth, which is then reactivated by simply washing the garment," the underwear company promises on its website.

"Here at Shreddies we firmly believe that everybody should own a pair of these amazing undies. The average person passes wind 14 times per day so whether you're a sufferer of a digestive disorder or just have flatulence, Shreddies can help."

"Anybody that suffers from excessive flatulence will know of the social issues that it can cause and Shreddies not only improves the physical symptoms but also helps reduce the anxiety associated with this condition," their website says. "In many cases, simply not having to worry about flatulence can help improve a persons condition."

Just how good Shreddies will be in filtering out the odor from long farts remains to be seen. There is a record of the longest fart ever let, and Shreddies may not be able to deal with such bombast.

The Guinness Book of World Records claims the longest fart fart was cut by Bernard Clemmens, who hailed from London, England. He sustained a fart of 2 minutes and 42 seconds.

There is no mention of how many pints of Guinness Mr. Clemmens had to drink first to prepare for his record breaking counter belch. Nor do we know who officially recorded this gaseous statement. Did they simply use a stopwatch and a microphone?

Furthermore, did the fart begin with a bang and end with a whimper? From our long experience with farts we conclude the two best instruments to measure the length and intensity of a fart are the ear and the nose.

Unofficially, Mr. Methane did record live from Paris what he claims to be the worlds longest fart. A video camera, a microphone and an iPhone were used in the documentation. Watch the video to see and hear for yourself. Without smell-a-vision, it's hard to say if this is a real fart or more Hollywood special effects.

When all is said and done, the fart and its aftermath seems to have a hold on our memory. What author would not like to share in this hold and have his work remembered through the ages? Perhaps the fart offers all story tellers such an opportunity. A fellow writer, Pete Cholewinski, reminded me how long our memories are when it comes to farts. It is fitting, in the end, that we recall one of the stories from the Tales from the Thousand and One Nights, aptly called, "The

Historic Fart." In this story a rich merchant decides to marry. At the marriage feast, he has a great deal to eat and drink. When he was summoned to the bridal chamber, he rose to his feet and "let go a long and resounding fart." People pretended nothing happened, but he was so embarrassed he left town and lived in India for ten years.

One day, homesick for his friends, he decided to disguise himself and return. Hoping time would erase the memory of his wedding night, he went around the outskirts of town. As he sat down to rest at the door of a hut, he heard the voice of a young girl within, saying: "Please, mother what day was I born on? One of my friends wants to tell my fortune."

"My daughter," replied the women solemnly, "you were born on the very night of Abu Hasan's fart." To his dismay, Abu Hasan realized his fart would be remembered till the end of time. We do not know what happened to Abu Hasan after that fateful encounter. It is comforting to think this episode taught him something of our common humanity, and he went on with his life. When we look the fart squarely in its brown eye, we see ourselves looking back. We should not become afraid or revolted at this discovery, for as President

Harry Truman once said, "Things work out for the best in the end."

What Is a Fart?

Thanks to the exhaustive research of a Minneapolis gastroenterologist, Dr. Michael Levitt (highlighted in the April 1995 issue of Discover Magazine, by Jeffrey Kluger), much has been learned about the humble fart. According to the above article, "Doctor Levitt's clinical fascination with farts began in 1976, when he encountered a patient afflicted with what he noted was "a five-year history of passing excessive flatulence." Having no data or available standards on what constituted excessive flatulence, other than family, friends, and associates of the patient (It seems my little book had not yet reached Minnesota), Dr. Levitt deemed it a worthy void to be filled. His 19 years of extensive analysis have uncovered the following:

--Flatulence is the body's way of purging the colon of unwanted gases and relieving pressure on the intestines. This gas, and pressure from same, is the result of (a) what we eat (b) air ingested while we eat and (c) the chemical interactions of the food with a variety of microbes that inhabit our lower tract. Experimentation and study rendered up some general baselines for flatulence, and are as follows:

--average episodes of flatulence per person is 13.6 per day

--average release of gas per episode is between 35-90 milliliters, averaging 500 - 2,000 milliliters per day

--flatulence is gender and ethnically neutral; affirmative action and flatulence distribution for the disadvantaged is unnecessary, as no one is flatulence impaired

--99% of what makes up flatulence is both odorless and colorless (carbon dioxide, hydrogen, nitrogen, oxygen and methane)

--microorganisms in the digestive tract take what they need during the digestive process, in turn generating waste of their own, in the form of gas

--while variances in individual metabolisms can explain why some can "pass" without notice and others can reverse an Amtrak commuter train, it's what is eaten that plays a large part in the adding the 'spritz' that gave rise to the phrase, "silent but deadly."

--foods containing complex carbohydrates--made up of three or four different sugar molecules--are among the worst offenders in creating flatulence, as well as a distinctive olfactory exclamation point."

Of course, anyone who knows human beings knows that the true meaning of the fart cannot be captured by the primitive net of scientific description. The fart is a creature both strong and weak, mighty and humble, a true creature of our imagination. In truth the fart is all and nothing. It is the test of our philosophy and the butt of our jokes. The fart forces us to seek our freedom and hold our breath. If you wish to know mankind, then learn all you can about the fart.

The Essence of Bean, Part 2

Dear Cecil:

Your recent discussion of farts and beans is somewhat misleading. I would like to call your attention to a paragraph from my monograph, "A Metaphysical and Anecdotal Consideration of the Fart" (Alphabeta Press). "Little did we know as children about the power and symbolism of beans. If we had read The White Goddess by Robert Graves, we would have known that beans were filled with wondrous powers and ought not be mocked. Graves tells us in his book that the Pythagorean mystics were bound by a strong taboo against eating beans. To eat beans was to eat one's parents' heads. This superstition was similar to the views held by the Platonists. They excluded beans on the rationalistic ground that they caused flatulence. Life, they argued, was breath, and to break wind after eating beans was proof one had eaten a living soul." The point here is that the soul is associated with breath, you know, "pneuma," pneumonia, etc, and that a fart was a kind of breath, so a soul was created and escaped, etc.

Thus the connection with reincarnation. If you are going to consider this subject in your column, why won't you answer the many letters I have sent you in the past about fish farts? If you recall, I wanted to know if in fact fish fart. As a woman who has spent much time at sea, I still have no answer to this question. Your attention to this matter will help me finish my monograph on the subject.

--Gloria Klein, via the Internet

Cecil replies:

"Gloria, I'm not sure which is the more troubling thought: (1) This letter is a joke, or (2) it isn't."

FLATULENCE:
The Downside of Global Warming

There is much debate now about the cause of global warming. Some even question whether or not global warming is actually happening. Nevertheless, you can't attend a cocktail party in Chicago's trendy Lincoln Park neighborhood without the subject of global warming coming up.

Green house gasses, automobiles, abuse of the environment by U. S. corporations: all these have been offered as reasons for global warming. Even cow flatulence is a cause of worry for some because cows spend about 8 hours a day passing gas. Furthermore, there are so many cows and their emissions are mostly methane. Methane is estimated to be about 20 times more potent than carbon dioxide as a cause of global warming.

Termites are also a source of worry for a few scientists who study global warming because termites emit methane, too, and are so numerous in some parts of the world. Termite flatulence may account for as much global warming as fossil fuel burning. Eating wood all day does put a lot of fiber in your diet, even if one scientist interviewed at the University of Chicago claimed, "That theory stinks!"

Termites and cows may be a reason for concern, but why do we avoid what is right before our nose--human beings? Why is it that human flatulence seems not to be mentioned as a cause of global warming? Is this an example of political correctness ignoring the facts? Human flatulence may be the key to understanding why our summers seem to be growing hotter. To look at global warming from the bottom up, is to break new wind on the subject.

Although some people claim they never pass gas, estimates are that the average person does so about 14 times a day, producing about 7 liters of gas. Most flatulence comes from swallowed air and consists largely of nitrogen and carbon dioxide. It is this carbon dioxide, mixed with small amounts of methane, that is a cause of worry, not only in a crowded elevator but world wide.

Seven liters of gas per person can multiply into a serious amount of gas let into the global atmosphere. Some scientist argue that it was the tremendous amounts of dinosaur flatulence that actually led to their extinction. A few moments meditation on the gut of a brontosaurus can persuade one of that theory.

The two nations responsible for most of the human flatulence in the world today are India and China. The population of India is estimated to be 1.09 billion people, while the population of China is estimated to be 1.3 billion. Together they have more that 2.5 billion people. That's 17.5 billion liters of gas passing into the atmosphere each day. You do the math!

Even though the U. S. population recently reached 300 million, when it come to flatulence, we have not been holding our own, either. Over the course of a year, the sum total of gas from our gut released into the atmosphere worldwide is significant, yet you never hear any discussion about this at the U. N.

Besides population, diet is another contributing factor to so much flatulence coming from India and China. People in these countries eat a diet mainly of vegetables, legumes and grains, all of which contribute to flatulence. These countries are also too poor for many to afford Beano, a product used in the environmentally conscious West to diminish flatulence.

If we are worried about global warming and its consequence for the next generation, then we must do at least two things to diminish human flatulence. Policies must be put in effect to reduce the population of both India and China, and at the same time we must institute changes in their diet. We must do this while there is still time to prevent the polar ice caps from melting.

Wake up World! Because it is ignored, human flatulence may be the end of us all. If the association of green house gasses with global warming is an inconvenient truth for Al Gore, then certainly the contribution of human flatulence to global warming is an incontinent truth.

Food for Thought

"You think you can steal my shit?"

—OJS

As it happens, the Chicago Red Line subway train is careening through the tunnel towards the Harrison stop when a young man who is sitting next to where I stand, suddenly jumps up and asks me, "Is this where I get down for Columbia College?"

I had noticed this undergraduate earlier as he sat next to his mother. She wore a colorful sari and their complexions allowed me to fantasize that he was a student showing his mother around Chicago. When I heard his question, I knew from my days living in Calcutta they were both recently arrived from India.

"Yes, this is the stop," I say. They both quickly move through the crowd and exit. The doors close and the train jerks forward. Too bad I didn't have time to explain the difference between "getting off" and "getting down," those who are native to Chicago take for granted.

Then, as I walk up the Roosevelt Station stairs to the street, it dawns on me the differences between getting off and getting down are more subtle than I first imagined. How would I explain to this young man in front of his mother if he goes to a gay bar Saturday night and meets someone he might "get off," but if he goes to a dance bar and gets into the music then he can "get down?" What a bit of mercury this English is.

Walking home in the rain, I see my neighbors are also out walking their dogs. One of the dogs stops, hunches back and lets fall his daily deposit on the lawn near my condo. Dutifully, the dog's master bends down and with a plastic bag on his hand scoops up the poop and deposits it in the corner trash can. I didn't want to see this brown tongue before dinner.

I purposely came this way because I wanted to avoid the small park where many of my neighbors walk their dogs, yet here they are, even when I take a different route. I had a personal encounter at that park that left a bitter taste in my mouth. I used to jog there, but such great quantities of dog droppings were deposited on the lawns, it constantly soiled my track shoes. I had to use a tooth brush to remove it from the cleats. Then, it took me a week to get the funny taste out of my tooth brush.

As I go up the elevator to my apartment, I realize what I did not want to see was actually a revelation. It was food for thought disguised. If the difference between getting off and getting down are difficult to explain, the many forms and uses of the English word "shit" are ever so more complex. I decide, in the interest of improving foreign understanding, to compile some notes about the uses of "shit" and its many meanings. As a public service, I can turn these notes into a little pamphlet, and leave it anonymously on the train for future tourists to read.

When it comes to explaining shit, especially to foreigners, you soon realize most people don't know shit. First of all, we must recognize that shit is a second place swear word in English. That's probably why it's use has been overlooked as a topic of an essay. The most offensive and obscene word in the English language is "fuck." Because of this, fuck has been given extensive academic and humorous treatment. How ironic shit has taken a back seat to fuck, or to borrow a line from the poet W. B. Yeats: "Love has pitched its tent in the place of excrement."

It's not that shit is used less than fuck when Chicagoans speak. It's just that shit does not carry the same power and electricity as fuck. We say, for example, "Fuck that shit!" I never heard anyone in Chicago say, "Shit that fuck!" Perhaps the best use of fuck that seems almost impossible to translate into Korean is the English curse I saw first on a T shirt in New Orleans, "Fuck you, you fucking fuck." Substituting the word shit here makes little sense or impact.

Even if shit isn't as powerful a word as fuck, it does its duty and we have many uses for it as a noun, verb and adjective. The subtleties of usage are almost as fine as those that some claim can be tasted in vintage wines. If you can flavor your speech with the correct use of shit, then you can go from being a foreigner in Chicago to being a real American. This transformation certainly requires more from the speaker than just the straightforward expression, "Shit, get off that fuckin' ladder."

Shit is a vulgar word in Modern English denoting feces. It's a native English word, and for many native speakers in

Chicago, shit is used as an abstract noun which refers to an almost endless number of things. In fact, we can use the word shit as a replacement for the word "thing." "This shit's bad," is a good example of such a replacement. So is the sentence, "I know about street shit, I just don't know all that legal shit."

What we mean here is urban uses of the word shit. My colleague who lives near the upper peninsula of Michigan reminds me there is a rural shit that we urbanites overlook. He maintains there are expressions that use turkey shit, wolf shit, elk shit, skunk shit, deer shit, and rabbit shit. There is also "the shitting in the woods by the sloping foreheaded, cedar savage dumb ass redneck knuckle dragging locals, who live in trailers that are rejects from the local trailer parks." How about that shit!

Other forms of the word shit are shitty, shitted and shat. We seldom use shat anymore as a past tense. The simple, straight forward shit is now the word of choice. When it comes to the adjective shitty, even that can be turned into shit. Instead of saying "Jim has a shitty car," we can quite easily say, "Jim's car is shit."

Shit also carries a variety of figurative meanings. Perhaps the most common are generic expressions of displeasure as in simply "Shit!" Fear or surprise when we open the door and see a werewolf standing there or we drop our grandmother's crystal bowl encourages us to say "Oh, shit!" or "Holy shit!" "Holy shit, Batman!" is a twentieth century example of shit Victorians may not understand.

When shit is used as a comparative noun, as in "This essay is a piece of shit," it can be applied to many parts of the universe. Most of the time when in an urban environment we use the word shit to refer simply to shit, we make reference to either bovine, equestrian, avian or human shit.

In the scale of shit, human shit is the most offensive and bird shit is the least offensive, except when it comes to calling someone who is afraid to jump from the swimming pool's highest diving board, chicken shit. Bullshit is a commonly used expletive, but whale shit or spider shit is seldom used as an expression in our urban culture.

Sometimes, we say horseshit as equal to bullshit as in "The Democrats' argument to end the war is horseshit," but most of the time when we make something equal to shit, we mean human shit. It's the intimate connection between humanity and shit in Chicago that confuses many foreigners.

Take for example someone who doesn't give a shit. Who comes to mind? The mayor? Your father? That one who slept with you last week, but never called you back? Sometimes, these people don't give a fuck, either, but most likely they just don't give a shit. But now here is where a confusion may arise for many recently arrived from South Asia. What is the difference between to give a shit and to take a shit?

When Mary asks at the office, "Where is Abdula?" and someone replies, "He went to take a shit," we know that in truth Abdula really GIVES a shit. It would strike us odd if Abdula actually waited in the bathroom for someone to leave a stall and then went to an unflushed toilet, reached down into the water, separated the floating tissue and took out a strand of shit, then went back to work. When Abdula goes to the shithouse he gives a shit to the toilet. Anything else proves he's a dipshit. Such are the wonders of language and the transformation of words by the unconscious.

What possible explanation is there for saying "to take a shit" when in fact we give a shit? The explanation that appeals to most analysts is one that makes reference to the unconscious mind and the roots language has in the unconscious. Most people recognize in our culture there is much guilt associated with bodily functions, especially those functions that expel matter and fluid from the body. To let lose piss and shit and phlegm are to do dirty things. In turn, we are made dirty by them.

Furthermore, we lose something of ourselves when we expel these things from our body. By pissing and shitting we are made less. When we combine this feeling of loss with the feeling of guilt in an expression where language attempts to make up for what is missing while at the same time assuaging our guilt, "to give a shit," is transmuted by the unconscious to "to take a shit." When we go to take a shit by giving a shit we tell everyone we have overcome our sense of loss and our feeling of guilt.

Believe it or not, there is poetry in shit, just as most poetry read at open mikes is shit. Many believe no computer yet built can understand the shaded nuances of this four letter word. Jonathan Swift was no Robert Browning, but Swift did have an eye for the brown. In his famous poem, "The Lady's

Dressing Room," Swift bluntly reminds us that love, no matter how ideal, is grounded in the realities of the body. Swift writes, "Thus finishing his grand Survey/Disgusted Strephon stole away/Repeating in his amorous Fits/Oh! Celia, Celia, Celia shits!"

Dung is a nice word. It has the poetic sound of a bell about it. Likewise, honeypot is a pleasant euphemism for shitholes, but words for shit lose something when they become delicate. Rather large boots are shitkickers. Shithooks may refer to idiots or more often hands, as in "Get your shithooks off me!" On occasion we can use the word shit twice in the same sentence as when a police officer arrests a purse snatcher and the woman maintains, "He's the shithead who needs the shit kicked out of him!" Both mothers disciplining their children and surgeons in the operating room may use the expression, "Cut that shit out!"

Just because shit is nuanced does not mean it helps us discern a complex truth. On the one hand, if someone were to say, "I voted for this shit before I voted against it," we may well wonder at their veracity. On the other hand, I once imagined a grocery store where at the exit they posted a sign saying, "Everything we sell turns to shit." That would be truth in advertising we seldom see.

Shit is not always a bad thing, even when it hits the fan. I bet some of my readers have been to a gallery where you wanted to say an artist's abstract paintings are shit. Afterwards, you go to a party where some weed is passed around and with a long toke, you admit, "That's some good shit!" Your boyfriend, always the contrary one, echoes, "Man, that's some BAD shit!" Not to be outdone, the man across the coffee table trumpets, "This motherfuckin' shit's somethin' else, Jack!" On those rare occasions when something is very special, "motherfuckin'" is a good modifier for shit.

Language is electric and forever changing. This is especially the case with English spoken in an era of political correctness like the one we live in, now. Can we expect shit to lose some of its punch when it is outlawed like pate de foie gras? This may be already happening to fuck. In the mainly heterosexual expression, where Jason, caught up in anger because his wife Heather maxed out the credit card says, "You fucking cunt!" the gerund seems to have lost part of its charge to the noun. Some gays, however, while sipping cosmos, hear this expression, shrug their shoulders and think, who gives a shit.

Knowing how to use shit is an art in itself. Having a taste for it is another matter. Does chocolate come to mind here? Mandel Hall and Dan Sabbath write in their treatise, END PRODUCT, "The sight of peanut butter, the smell of cheese are not the only giveaway to our desire. Sausages and chitterlings are made from the original shitbags. Terrified as we are of the turd, most of us remain unaware of its tastiness."

Except when you are in the army and learn that cooks don't take shit from anyone but dish it out to everyone. You also learn in the barracks or perhaps at the movies that before you confront an obnoxious enemy and pop the cap on him, you exclaim, "Eat shit, asshole!" With this wonderful and compact reference to the rectum dentata we are brought back in a circle to where we started.

We should advise all visitors to Chicago as they start their tour that here you can be shitfaced, be shit out of luck, or have shit for brains, but with a little effort you can get your shit together, rent an apartment and find a place for your shit.

In spite of this, some people can't tell the difference between shit and Shinola. If you stay the summer or winter here you will learn quickly that some days are hotter than shit while others are colder than shit. I know. I read your thoughts: that's some weird shit.

There is so much more to be said for shit, over and above, or should I say under and below its colloquial usage. Shit is food for thought, because food is nothing more than the golden end of shit. Like troubles among the poor, we can safely say, "There's no end to this shit." These days, because we often learn metaphysics from reading bumper stickers, we know, too, that "Shit happens." Add to that, shit's profound and fundamental meaning, anyone who wants to live in Chicago better know their shit or they'll end up in deep doodoo. If foreigners are helped in their understanding of our subtle Chicago expressions, I am grateful. What better place than by a pamphlet on the Brown Line train to learn a taste for life and life's many shades? They say all the world's on a train. Shit, ain't it the truth.

Appendix on One Sheet of Toilet Tissue

The pop singer Sheryl Crow's recent contention that only one sheet of toilet tissue is necessary after using the bathroom finds many sitting in wonder. In fact, her recommendation has a long history. The green and the brown have gone hand in hand for centuries. When we look at the world from the bottom up, we soon learn that what is new is really old.

Living outside the U. S. taught many of us to be frugal to the point where Sheryl Crow may be viewed as being excessive in her use of just one sheet. The goal of our frugality in India was to live like a character in Heinrich Böll's book GROUP PORTRAIT WITH LADY. Böll has a character, one very frugal nun, who believes that a truly healthy person doesn't need any paper at all after doing their duty.

If you can't be like that nun, then here are directions on how to use the minimum: Take one sheet of tissue and fold it in half, then fold it in half again and again. You should be left with what looks like a triangle of paper. Gently tear off about a half inch of paper from the top, pointed end. Save this small piece. You will need it later.

Now, unfold the paper. You should have a square with a hole in the center big enough to insert your left hand pointer finger.

Insert your finger in the paper's hole. Approach the area that needs wiping. With a circular motion, do your cleanup, and then with your right hand, slip off the tissue from your finger, cleaning the finger as you slide upward. Discard the used toilet tissue.

Finally, take the small piece you saved torn from the tip, and use it to clean your fingernail.

Halfway into our tour of India we ran out of toilet paper altogether. We were forced to search the local market for a replacement and discovered airmail stationary. I can report that this stationary was crisp but reliable, something an e-mail never will be.

Yellow Snow:
The Impact of Dog Piss on the Urban Environment

The Quantity and Distribution of Dog Piss (1)

If you or I went into the street, then opened our clothes and pissed, our neighbors would be shocked and moved to action. "How could you do that?" they would ask. Nevertheless, dogs piss in the street every day and most of us are blind to it. We accept it as a natural part of urban life. No one seems to care about it.

We should care, because the diseases dog piss spreads, and the destruction of buildings and structures it perpetuates is a silent menace to civilized urban life. If we don't do something about dog piss soon, we may find the city crumbling around us. This paper attempts to investigate the problem of dog piss in urban areas and offer some solutions.

There are over 50 million dogs in this country alone, costing their owners $5 billion a year in dog food. Needles to say this food turns to waste and has to be disposed. About $7 billion a year is spent in veterinary care and $250 million in insurance claims for the 800,000 people bitten seriously enough to warrant medical attention.

With these figures in mind, just imagine how much dog piss is deposited on our streets every day. In a crowed urban neighborhood like the South Loop in Chicago, where the number of dogs is great, the cumulative effect over the course of a year is prodigious. It has been estimated that in a normal South Loop block there are more than one hundred and fifty apartments. With a dog owner rate of twelve percent, that is more than eighteen dogs per block. This could mean more than two hundred dogs in the neighborhood. Each of those dogs piss daily on our streets and lawns.

Estimates of the amount of dog piss released into the environment are hard to come by due to such variables as the size of the dog, its health and age. Certainly it seems logical that a sound Saint Bernard would piss more that an old poodle. If we accept the estimate of an average dog urination at three ounces, and if a normal dog pisses twice a day, that is six ounces of dog piss per dog per day. Over the course of a year an urban neighborhood can be flooded by more that seven thousand gallons of dog piss. It doesn't take an expert in urology to see that the effect of this amount of corrosive waste can have devastating environmental impact.

The Chemical Composition of Dog Piss

The chief components of dog piss are water, urea, dissolved minerals and salts along with bacteria and other infectious agents. The quantities of these components vary, with water making up about eighty percent of the total volume of most piss deposits. Urea makes up about fifteen percent of the total volume, and is considered by chemists to be the most dangerous component in dog piss. Urea reacts with such things as aluminum, steel and sand, and corrodes them. Urea's corrosive effects are enhanced by heat and sunlight. The remaining five percent are inert matters, salts, minerals and infectious organisms that create their own problems.

The Corrosive Effects of Dog Piss on Stone, Concrete and Metal Structures

When dog piss reacts with concrete, metal or stone it can have a devastating and destructive effect.(2) Great quantities of dog piss over long periods of time actually dissolve the foundations of buildings.(3) Dog piss can likewise eat away at the bolts and fasteners that hold up signs and other metal structures. Man's best friend is destroying the city in which we have achieved the heights of cultural and social evolution. If we do not limit the amount of dog piss rained on our fire hydrants, sign posts, corner stones and side walks, we will have to replace these structures, along with the buildings themselves, in a matter of years. Can we afford the long term consequences of the damage done by dog piss when there are so many other pressing urban problems?

Evaporated Dog Piss and the Urban Atmosphere

Besides destroying building foundations and other structures, evaporating dog piss adds to air pollution and the spread of diseases.(4) How many people, unknowingly step in puddles of fresh piss on the sidewalk and transport microbes into their homes, where they bread in carpets. The Eastern custom of not wearing shoes in the house seems to be good advice, in light of the amount of dog piss on the streets in some urban areas.

On a hot day in a crowded city, the amount of evaporated dog piss in the air is enough to cause eye irritation, coughing and exposure to other diseases. Alicia del Perro argues that Mexico City would be better off without dogs. We feel that every city in the United States, especially their central business district, would be better off without dogs as well.

Remedies, Regulations and Suggestions Regarding Dog Piss

The most effective way to solve the problem of dog piss in the urban environment is to kill all the dogs now here, and not allow anymore on the streets. To this end we encourage adopting the Vietnamese and Korean custom of eating dog meat.

If we cannot get immediate dog killings, then our next objective is to regulate their number and license them. State Senator Rich Water's proposal to charge a high fee for a dog pissing license, followed by strict prosecution of those dogs caught pissing without one, will discourage dog ownership. An effective Piss Patrol could be funded out of the licensing fees. We support the efforts of the Senator in this regard.

Barricades, irritating chemicals and guards could also be placed in areas most frequented by pissing dogs. We suggest small packets of powerful dog poison be placed as well.(5) These may be obtained by writing our organization. Address your requests to Kathy Collie, National Secretary, PUPPY, 16 Bull Dog Road, Canine, New York, 10035, or call 1-800-DOG-GONE.

Probably the least effective measure to decrease dog piss in the urban environment is to establish DDA's (Dog Depletion Areas), special places in parks and on streets set aside for dog pissing.(6) This will concentrate dog piss in one area which later can be regularly disinfected and neutralized. (7)

Recently research has been conducted in an attempt to train dogs to piss in a designated area. So far, the results have been inconclusive.(8) This does not solve, however, the problem of an abundance of dogs. Our organization sees

DDA's as a token measure. It is a case of barking up the wrong tree. In fact, DDA's give into dog owners and encourage public pissing. PUPPY, People United to Prevent Public Pissing, is against all animal or human pissing in public. In another paper we will discuss the effects of drunks, vagrants and homeless people pissing in our streets and alleys. (9) At the moment, dogs still remain the major culprit. Our hope is to solve this problem before tackling others.

END NOTES

(1) It is important to distinguish dog piss from wolf and fox piss. We do not want especially to exclude the latter. Tablets soaked in wolf or fox piss are an aid to gardeners. Selectively placed around the garden, they can discourage squirrels and chipmunks from eating the crops.

Just because we focus our attention on dog piss does not mean we want to ignore the environmental impact of dog shit. This is another problem for urban dwellers which has reached crisis proportions. For a detailed analysis of this crisis see Hayakawa Jujitzu, "Hono Bono Katazume," Tokyo Today, Vol. 10, No. 7, April 1989. pp. 17-28.

Dog shit, a byproduct of dog food, continues to clog our streets, too. For a complete analysis of what dog food tastes like and what it is made from, see Ann Hodgman's article, "No Wonder They Call Me a Bitch," in Spy, 1989. She subjects the leading brands of dog food to a taste test in her own kitchen and discloses startling results.

Furthermore, in a letter from the Chicago Department of Streets and Sanitation to the President of the 901 Condominium Association, Eileen J. Carey reports on the difficulties her office has in controlling rats around the buildings of the South Loop. She writes, "Although you are correct that trash disposal is generally under control in the area, we found numerous instances where dog feces were plentiful—including around the exterior of the 901 building. There is no question the unwillingness of dog owners to pick up after their pets is the major cause of the rat problem; rats can and do survive on this material, at least half of which is undigested food."

(2) Dr. M.T. Bladder, "Korozion von Urin," Urology, Vol. 22, No. 6, Stockholm, Sweden, November, 1989, pp. 8-12.

(3) Rajit Singh, "Hindu Dogs?" Bihar Times, Vol. 88, No. 2, March 12th, 1986. According to this article, a porch collapsed in the city of Jamshedpur. It was attached to a house owned by a Sikh electrician. The police report concluded that the porch collapse was caused by structural failure. It seems that the many Hindus of the neighborhood let their dogs roam at will around the grounds of the owner and encouraged their pissing on the support columns. This is the first documented case of a structure being undermined by dog piss. In a related incident, on the other side of the world, dog piss was involved in a death by shooting. Christopher Merola, 21, was shot to death and two other people were wounded in a gun fight that broke out at Staten Island, New York. It seems the family dog urinated on the neighbor's bushes, beginning the battle.

(4) Alicia del Perro, "La contaminacíon del aire y agua en la capital," Revista de la Salud Publica, Mexico, D.F., 1990, Vol. 3, No. 6, pp. 28-33.

(5) If poisons are not readily available, chocolate or ibuprofen tablets will do. Dogs love both of them, and fortunately they are very toxic to dogs while safe for people. Just scatter bits of chocolate or ibuprofen tables around the park and watch the dogs gobble them up. Better yet, wrap the ibuprofen in bits of chocolate. Later, watch them keel over at the vets.

(6) Kirk Zeeland, "Hound Stool Gemessupt," Reich und Stadt, Vol. 12, No. 3, Amsterdam, 1989. According to Zeeland, the City of Amsterdam tried this solution and it proved to be a failure. Dog owners refused to use the special locations set aside for them, funded by volunteer donations.

(7) The village council of Bruntingthorpe, England, is working on an elaborate plan to reduce the amount of dog doo doo in the town of 200 people and 30 dogs. The village plans to give DNA tests to all the dogs and keep the results on file. DNA samples from the uncollected dog doo

doo found lying around would then be compared to the DNA samples on file to identify the scofflaws. The cost of this program makes it unlikely it will go over here in the States. Furthermore, the difficulty of obtaining reliable samples of dog piss makes it hard to do the DNA tracking. In the end, fido on the barbecue still looks like the best option.

(8) The Charlotte, North Carolina Observer reported in November 1994 that an Australian terrier named Willie stared in an experiment at Davidson College in which four students sprayed a dog-scented chemical on stakes, hoping to see how often dogs would urinate on the scent. Willie, who's legendary because he's been known to urinate dozens of times while strolling through the neighborhood, correctly hit three of the five marked stares. These number are just not acceptable for a crowded urban environment.

(9) A case in point can be read about in Windy City Times for July 9th, 1992. In Mother Superior's column, "Nasty Habits," we read about what happened at the gay pride parade because there was a lack of porta-toilets: "...many people were forced to visit the alleys to relieve themselves.... My girlfriend and I went to find a safe place in the alley and walked past a gay man who was responding to Mother Nature's call. We apologized to him and told him we wouldn't look.... We proceeded to talk about...politics and the community. Where else could you have two dykes squatting between dumpsters and a gay man holding his dick peeing, talking about politics?" Is this a nasty habit, or what?

According to another article in June, 1995 Southtown Economist, "Dogs giving their traditional one-legged salute are ruining a $20,000 sidewalk lighting system in Tiburon, Calif. Local officials are, in a word, peeved. The damage is costing the San Francisco Bay community $200 a month, town Public Works Director Tony Iacoppi said. The foot-tall lights on the Shoreline Park walkway are a magnet for canines in search of fire hydrants, he said. All it takes is one dog to pee on it, and then it's over. Every dog in the world wants to pee on them, he said. They are corroding all the fixtures and all the wiring. Town Manager Bob Kleinert says it may be cheaper in the long run to replace them with out-of-reach fixtures."

Gloria Klein is the National Director, PUPPY, (People United to Prevent Public Pissing)

Leave That Shit at Home

We take the L on the way home from the Printers Row Book Fair. Jonathan tells me a joke about two cannibals who are eating a comedian. One cannibal stops eating, turns to the other and asks, "Does this taste funny?"

After that, Jonathan describes the awful conditions under which he had to take a piss. I know right away he had a bad experience in one of those blue closets set up to take our bladder's confession.

Both of us cannot tolerate people who use the Port-a-Pottie for a dump instead of taking care of their number 2 business at home.

"There's one thing worse than cannibals eating a comedian, and that's leaving a load of shit in a Port-a-Pottie for the next person to see," Jonathan says with a look of disgust on his face. "Those blue closets are set up as a convenience to pee, not as a chance to unload. In Atlanta no one ever makes a deposit like that!"

"It's not polite," I say.

"Exactly! Just as a gentleman is a man who can play the accordion, but doesn't, so a considerate man is one who needs to poop in a Port-a-Pottie, but doesn't. You do that business before you leave your house."

"I know," I say in agreement. "When I went into the handicapped Port-a-Pottie, and tried to change my blouse, I was forced to undergo the same assault."

"Jeez," Jonathan adds, "Why can't those people do it at home?"

"The problem is, no matter when you go to pee, there's a pile of shit in them."

"They must ship them already loaded?" Jonathan speculates.

"Do some people plan their evacuation ahead of time?" I wonder.

"Like, they stuff themselves the night before on Hot Pockets, Mexican food and cabbage, the way a marathon runner eats a load of carbs before a big race."

I imitate my friend Bubba in New Orleans. ""Why you eatin' so much beans, Roger?' Bill asks. 'Cuz I goin' to the book fair tomorrow, and dey got one of dem Port-a-Potties der dat I just gotta use,' Roger answers with excitement. Bill nods approval and has another Hot Pocket himself, all the while thinking he could use the Port-a-Pottie next to Roger and they could have a farting contest."

"Why is it, no matter where you go these days, a rock concert in Lincoln Park, Halsted Street Days, even Ravinia; every Port-a-Pottie you enter always has at the bottom of the seat a smoldering hill of shit?" Jonathan asks.

"And it's not just a turd or two. It's always the glossy, soft kind of shit, sometimes as long as your arm. It just sits there, looking up at you like a lizard as you try to pee. What the hell, you think, when did this shit happen?"

"It's not just 'when,' but 'who.'"

"It's gotta be a meat eater," I insist.

"Tiger shit always smells worse than elephant shit."

"Do you think it's the homeless?"

"Probably not, they don't get that much meat to eat," Jonathan replies as if he knows what he's talking about.

"A bike messenger? Dude, outa my way! I gotta delivery to make."

"I always try to aim my pee way from it," Jonathan says advisedly.

"You gotta wonder why can't they do that shit before they leave the house? I mean, leave the load at home!"

"I think its got a lot to do with bran," Jonathan says, expecting me to agree. "Some people have a bowl of bran for breakfast, then leave the house.

"They are unaware of bran's explosive potential."

"It goes through them, like a hot knife through butter," Jonathan adds, then makes a sweeping motion with his hand.

"Make sure your wrist watch is on tight. You don't want to drop your Rolex down there after they make a visit."

By now, people on the crowded L car are smiling at us. That doesn't stop Jonathan. "I knew a guy like that who did a number on my bathroom every time he came over to visit."

"No!"

"Yes! Five minutes after he comes through my front door he is sitting on my toilet, groaning. Regular as clockwork."

"Didn't he have a toilet at home?"

"Of course he did, but for some reason he had to leave his house and do it at mine."

"That's not right."

"Whatever happened to the "Three Ss: shit, shave and shower?" Jonathan asks. "You were supposed to do the Three Ss before you leave the house. You arrive at work smooth faced, clean and empty."

"Not any more," I tell Jonathan.

"Empty is just for gas tanks, now."

"It doesn't help, either, to know that up north the euphemism for a Port-a-Pottie is 'Honey Bucket,'" I say, and then turn to look out the window to see where we are.

"Like, dude, where's the honey?" Jonathan asks jokingly.

"It must be a 'man thing,' a way of marking territory."

"Maybe illegal immigrants are saving it up to get even."

"I don't care! What about the children? How do you explain that load of shit to a kid?"

"Tell 'em it was a dinosaur. Kids like dinosaurs."

"Or galactic Dream Whip from the Dark Side."

The L screeches it's way to Lake and State Street. I must transfer to the Green Line. Jonathan stays onboard. Before I get up to leave, we both agree, "Leave that shit at home!"

Shadow Play

This poem contains mediations on looking into the toilet bowl. Every morning for a month, the poet disciplined herself by writing down the first thought that came to mind after gazing on the results of her duty.

Dark matters.

Brown and bent as long as your arm.

Little pellets, my night stones.

Look, a beaver, curled up and asleep in the water!

Let the sewer gulp another gift.

Half hidden--lurking like a crocodile.

I waited. It was supposed to appear after breakfast, but stalled.

Old tree limb, tossed by the rapids.

Wrapped in white, my brunette daughter finally leaves home.

Second movement, in F minor.

Hooked serpent, lost in the foam.

Let fish make a bed from this wood.

A queen washes only her finger tips.

Go, water searcher, tapered like a root.

Two guests and one host wait for the flood.

The whirlpool is in me, then in the flushing.

A Zen master writes of peanut butter.

Sounds of water running faint, like conscience.

The gods of mud and chocolate were lovers last
night.

If this were my only message to the
underworld.

First, second, turd.

Brown beef makes another stew.

Yesterday's Brahman becomes today's
Untouchable.

First the chill, then the stupor, then the letting
go.

Two: one long another short. My morning
exclamation!

This tan finger points where?

Burnt bamboo in the snow.

Bye, bye Miss American pie.

Yellow banana then, beige banana now.

The fart is greater than the hole.

Gloria Klein

Gloria Klein